What FAMILIES Say about
. . . . *The Truth about College Admissi*

"I read The *Truth about College Admission* in March while our high s____
to hear from her choices. This puts me about two years too late. I winced at where I got it wrong and felt lucky where I got it right. Clark and Barnard have combined their considerable experience to craft a guide that is witty and wise, profound and practical, funny and full of heart. They keep the focus on the essential questions in an effort to convert the college experience into something bold and wonderful—a celebration of family. This book will be my gift for friends who have children starting their college adventure."
—**MICHAEL K-D.**, parent, Saint Paul, MN

"Who knew a college admission book could be so enjoyable *and* provide pertinent information? This is exactly what I found. Clark and Barnard's perspective, mixing facts with humor, helped reduce my own stress and gave me a much-needed reality check. *The Truth about College Admission* is an outstanding resource for families, as it thoughtfully addresses the journey of college admission from beginning to move-in day." —**TINSLEY H.**, parent, Peachtree Corners, GA

"We could tell our sixteen-year-old was anxious about the college admission process. So we determined to make it a fun family activity: we agreed to meet once a week on Saturdays over cookies and tea to chat, ask questions, and explore ideas. What had been a dreaded topic became an enjoyable activity that she directed. We learned more in that first family conversation than we had over the previous several months of what seemed to her to be painful cross-examinations. This book is a godsend." —**PAUL M.**, parent, Pasadena, CA

"Clark and Barnard's writing effortlessly blends wisdom and wit, honesty and insight. It has truly saved our family's sanity during our college admissions adventure."
—**GAIL AND LOREN S.**, parents, Atlanta, GA

"Every family approaching college applications should be armed with *The Truth about College Admission*. It begins with aligning expectations and establishing a game plan for success. Each chapter follows the process from discovery, to applications and responses, and provides questions and realignment exercises for each engagement. This book helped us make sense of the process and understand the results. It was the soothing balm we all needed." —**LINDA S.**, parent, New York, NY

"During the college admission process, we were overwhelmed by all the 'noise' out there. I longed for guidance that would lead us in a way that felt more thoughtful and conscious. Then I found this book. It gave us permission to trust our own instincts and know that we don't have to get caught up in hiring expensive college consultants and comparing our child's journey to all her peers. Because we had this book as a resource, my family has learned to step back, take a deep breath, and ask questions about what's really important to us. This book is my new go-to gift for the parent of every junior and senior in high school!"
—**KASEY M.**, parent, Wilton, NH

What PROFESSIONALS Say about
············ *The Truth about College Admission* ············

"At last, a book about the college admission process that doesn't promise secret tips for admission (hint—there are none!) but instead provides advice from two respected and experienced professionals. If families are looking for how to manage the college admission process in an ethical, thoughtful, student-centered way, this book provides an important road map written in a way that even the most reluctant student will find engaging."
—**THYRA L. BRIGGS,** Vice President for Admission and Financial Aid, Harvey Mudd College

"I love this book. It's packed with sensible advice and some wonderful questions. I highly recommend it." —**ETHAN SAWYER,** College Essay Guy

"A *must-read* for students applying to college and their parents! Come along and share the authors' meaningful personal and professional stories, which will help you think through the entire process, including why you are doing what you are doing and how to make it all less stressful. I recommend this book highly to the students and families with whom I work." —**NANCY BEANE,** Past President, National Association for College Admission Counseling

"Barnard and Clark make a stressful decision more sane, understandable, and educationally useful. This book is needed because misinformation and a cacophony of noise about college admission are hurting students." —**JEROME A. LUCIDO,** Executive Director, University of Southern California Center for Enrollment Research, Policy, and Practice

"The college admission ritual can be a joyful opportunity for reflection and discovery. With insight, empathy, and wit, Barnard and Clark empower families to tune out the noise, own the journey, and focus on what really matters in a lived college experience."
—**MARK MOODY,** Director of College Counseling, Shanghai American School, Puxi Campus

"In a field that is sometimes viewed as nearly as much art as science and often fraught with misinformation, Barnard and Clark provide expertise that is accurate, useful, and empathetic to the needs of applicants and their families. The book is a terrific resource for students and parents." —**GARY S. MAY,** Chancellor, University of California at Davis

"This approachable book, which includes a great diversity of professionals who provide observations and advice, feels like a real, extended conversation. Barnard and Clark have crafted a terrific collaboration from both sides of the admission desk. On an all-too-crowded bookshelf of 'how-to' manuals for college admission, this book offers a much-needed step-by-step journey to a successful outcome for students and their families."
—**WILLIAM T. CONLEY,** Vice President for Enrollment Management, Bucknell University

"We have allowed admission selectivity to become a proxy for quality when it comes to how we assess colleges and universities. Barnard and Clark help us remember that talented students and incredible universities, of all levels of selectivity, find their way to each other every year. The right combination of student and college can be transformative for both! This book is a much-needed resource for families." —**GARY CLARK,** Director of Undergraduate Admission, University of California at Los Angeles

The Truth about College Admission

The Truth about

COLLEGE

ADMISSION

A FAMILY GUIDE

TO GETTING IN AND STAYING TOGETHER

Brennan Barnard
and Rick Clark

JOHNS HOPKINS UNIVERSITY PRESS

Baltimore

© 2019 Johns Hopkins University Press
All rights reserved. Published 2019
Printed in the United States of America on acid-free paper
9 8 7 6 5 4 3 2 1

Johns Hopkins University Press
2715 North Charles Street
Baltimore, Maryland 21218-4363
www.press.jhu.edu

Library of Congress Cataloging-in-Publication Data

Names: Barnard, Brennan E., 1974– author. | Clark, Rick, 1974– author.
Title: The truth about college admission : a family guide to getting in and
    staying together / Brennan Barnard and Rick Clark.
Description: Baltimore : Johns Hopkins University Press, [2019] | Includes
    bibliographical references and index.
Identifiers: LCCN 2019013426 | ISBN 9781421436371 (pbk. : alk. paper) |
    ISBN 142143637X (pbk. : alk. paper) | ISBN 9781421436388 (electronic) |
    ISBN 1421436388 (electronic)
Subjects: LCSH: Universities and colleges—United States—Admission. |
    College choice—United States.
Classification: LCC LB2351.2 .B37 2019 | DDC 378.1/610973—dc23
LC record available at https://lccn.loc.gov/2019013426

A catalog record for this book is available from the British Library.

Special discounts are available for bulk purchases of this book. For more information, please contact
Special Sales at 410-516-6936 or specialsales@press.jhu.edu.

Johns Hopkins University Press uses environmentally friendly book materials, including
recycled text paper that is composed of at least 30 percent post-consumer waste, whenever
possible.

*For our friend Denis Gainty, whose joyful curiosity and
dedication to always asking "why?"
lives on in connection and spirit*

Contents

Preface

In many homes and families around our nation, the discussion surrounding college begins in elementary school. With one eye on their own children, parents are also closely looking around their community. At work, on the soccer field, and at dinner parties, stories of high school seniors "getting in" to or "getting rejected" from one college or another add to the growing consternation.

By the time middle school rolls around, the stakes seem high. "Which classes do 'we' need to take?" "Should our daughter volunteer in an orphanage abroad or attend a computing camp this summer?" "Is it true that Eagle Scouts have a better chance of being admitted to an Ivy League school?"

Loving parents simply want their kids to have choices, options, and a happy, successful life. However, with understandably high hopes and expectations, parents often hinge future success on their children being admitted to a small subset of top-ranked and selective colleges. Entering and progressing through high school with this mentality can create a pressure cooker for families that leads to a constant focus and comparison of the number of Advanced Placement (AP) courses, SAT scores, achievements, awards, and titles, all in the name of "standing out" or "being enough" for college applications. Left unchecked, over time, especially as students enter their final two years of high school, this dynamic can result in acute fissures in the family because the singular focus becomes "getting in." *The Truth about College Admission* is meant to help you stay together as a family through this experience.

This book is written to put the college search and admission experience in perspective for your family. It challenges the common narrative that college admission is a rite of passage to fear and reclaims the opportunity many students and families often miss—one that provides growth, discovery, and excitement for the future. It runs counter to a few of the constant claims purported by the media: that there are only 25 great schools in our nation, that students have no chance of getting into a "good school," and that they must perfectly follow a secret formula throughout high school to unlock success.

In this book, students and their families will find insights and tips but no tricks; metaphors and analogies will help frame why and how admission decisions are made, but there will be no promises or guarantees of acceptance to particular schools. No shortage of "how to" books claim to uncover the "secret" to getting into college. This is the guide for the rest of us—parents and students who are intent on putting family first by engaging in real, healthy, balanced conversations. We will bring you laughs and smiles and, more importantly, encourage students to think deeply about why they are going to college. Answering *why* naturally leads them to *where* they should visit, apply, and ultimately go in order to grow, learn, and thrive in and beyond their college years, both as a student and as a family.

Most books on this subject are written by visiting journalists glancing in from the outside; or they are incomplete "tell alls" penned by former short-term staff members at competitive, private colleges; or they are by parents purporting to be experts because their child was admitted to an Ivy League school. These narratives fan the flames engulfing the frenetic college admission conversation—perpetuating the myth that there are tricks, insider information, and foolproof ways to avoid devastating pitfalls in the college admission experience that can only be mastered by reading so-called expert advice. They claim they have a corner on the market for the "winning essay" or know the perfect combination of extracurricular activities to get a scholarship or a coveted seat at a highly selective university. Families are continually receiving solicitations from high priced "consultants" or independent agents who charge exorbitant fees for "5-star essays" and promise to "open the doors to the nation's best colleges." The truth is that there is no blueprint or bona fide pathway to a specific place. Ultimately, the secret is that there is no secret, but there can be sanity—there can be unity.

Our guide is honest. It is based on a combined four decades of work in the field directly counseling and advising students and families in schools and communities. Using that experience, we outline why nobody can assure you a spot in selective colleges, and we describe how institutional priorities and school missions dictate decisions. Rather than laying out a *strategy* that can breed anxiety and exacerbate division, *The Truth about College Admission* debunks the myth that there is a script or a perfect formula for "standing out" or "getting in" and instead reframes the discussion about the wide landscape of American higher education. Interspersed with quotes from other veteran admission professionals, insight from thoughtful college leaders, and reflections from parents and students throughout our nation, this book provides anecdotes and perspective, questions and encouragement, options and hope that will help your family ultimately thrive—not just survive—during your college search and selection *experience*.

Authors' Note: As educators and admission professionals, we believe strongly in the power of higher education to transform lives and benefit both the individual and society, but we also acknowledge that the path to college is not for everyone. This book is written for students and families who have decided that pursuing a college degree is both valuable and important. Moreover, we focus our recommendations on traditional college-age students who are seeking four-year degrees. Our intention is to provide a guide for those navigating college admission that is more healthy and broad than we commonly see. We use the words *family* and *parents* as catchall terms to simplify the flow of our recommendations. We are aware, however, that families come in all shapes and sizes, and "parents" could refer to guardians, grandparents, or other trusted adults who are supporting young people through this experience. We want to honor the power of "family" as representing connection and community in helping students dream and plan for their future. We hope this guide will serve as a structure and resource for anyone engaging in the college search and application journey.

How to Use This Book

This book is designed to be a companion guide as you walk together through the college admission experience. It is intended to be a progressive resource that you can follow and refer to throughout your college search and application journey.

This guide is filled with both a contextual exploration of college admission and pragmatic resources and exercises that you can use along the way. Divided into four parts, it is designed to stimulate questions and promote dialogue. The first part is intended to set the stage for your college search. We provide suggestions on how best to approach the experience and what to expect from colleges and each other as a family. Chapter 1 begins by asking the important foundational question of *why* you are going to college and is followed in chapter 2 by a review of the current landscape in admission and how colleges search for students—dissecting the vast marketing budgets of schools and unpacking the robust strategies colleges and universities have for recruiting students. Chapter 3 explores some of the issues—or wedges—that commonly drive families apart if not approached intentionally or thoughtfully.

After setting the stage, in the second part of the book, we dive into the practical aspects of this experience. Chapter 4 incorporates contextual material from the preceding chapters to help you form a balanced college application list. We discuss the concept of "reach," "target," and "likely" schools while outlining the underlying premise that being admitted to any of these would be a great option. It explores in detail the notion of "match" and that the "right" school is not about its rank-ing but rather where a student is going to learn, grow, build a network, thrive inside and outside the classroom, and launch into life after col-lege. Next, chapter 5 discusses how to conduct a thorough campus visit. We provide questions to ask, people to see, and ways to maximize time and reflect on what you learned to inform your evolving college search. We will relate anecdotes and provide tips for parents and students so that they can avoid conflict and division. The chapter closes with quotes from parents and students about their experiences visiting a va-riety of colleges.

In the third part, chapters 6, 7, and 8 explore what colleges are look-ing for and how decisions are made, while addressing some of the pitfalls and best practices in applying to college. We take readers behind the scenes of college admission offices with discussions of ho-listic admission, institutional priorities, and how applications are re-viewed. This part pulls back the curtain and again humanizes admis-sion counselors and committees. Readers will be able to hear and better understand the ruminations, deliberations, and committee con-versations that occur as offices arrive at decisions and create their classes. It will provide nuance and context for what's happening after you submit the application. Who are these people on the other end? What takes so long for them to review and make a decision? The exploration will delve deep into each decision a student might re-ceive: admit, deny, defer, wait-list, and others. What does each one mean? What do you need to "do" next, if anything? We share our ex-tensive experience with a variety of different enrollment models, and these chapters include anecdotes and insight from admission deans and counselors.

Finally in the last part, chapters 9 and 10 provide practical guidance for making a final college choice that honors a mix of emotion and pragmatism. We propose a decision-making process that is grounded in honesty about desires, future, finances, and more. We also exam-ine the decision-making timeline, sometimes as compressed as three weeks in April, and how to do preemptive soul searching and research to be prepared when admission decisions and financial aid packages arrive. We focus on the critical need to "celebrate your success" to-gether with each college acceptance. Finally, acknowledging that this is a bittersweet time, we explore the concept of moving from parent to partner. We close with letters written to students and parents sep-

arately about how to make the most of this experience and to appreciate the role of family.

Just as the college admission experience is not to be approached passively, neither is this book. Our goal throughout is to help you remain
together, to provide perspective, and to challenge you to consider questions that will promote introspection and unity. At the end of each
chapter, you will find a Try This exercise that allows you to practice
what you have just learned. There are also questions to reflect on and
discuss in a Talk About This section that accompanies each chapter
and a brief Check In reminder to ensure that this journey remains
intentional. Are you on the same page? Are you excited about and encouraged to continue reading and considering the college experience?
If not, what do you need to do, discuss, or learn to get there?

 Our hope is that your family will take the time to engage with these
exercises and discussions, as they are designed to make your experience meaningful, uniting, and successful. Though these chapters are
presented sequentially, families will benefit from returning to various
chapters as references throughout the journey. So, lean in, check in,
and stay together as you experience this amazing adventure and journey as a family.

PART I

CHAPTER 1

Why Are You Going to College?

We thought we had all the answers.
It was the questions we had wrong.
"11 O'CLOCK TICK TOCK" BY U2

A family with generations of graduates from Georgia Tech had a daughter who had been denied admission. Her parents came to the admission office to appeal the decision. The father began, earnestly and restrained, "I just don't understand. She has all As. She is at the top of her class. Her test scores are great. When I got into Tech, I was not half as prepared as she is now. My test scores were average, and I'd never taken an Advanced Placement class in my life." As he began describing the activities she had participated in and the praise her teachers and coaches regularly lavished upon her, his hands started to clench. Periodically, he would bite his lower lip slightly and glance anxiously at his wife.

Meanwhile, the mother's head was down. Even though her brown hair was hanging on the table and hiding much of her face, I (Rick) could tell her eyes were now softly shut, perhaps in hopes she was anywhere but in my office right then. Their daughter was just staring straight ahead and shaking her head slowly. Then, for the first time, the father paused.

Momentary silence. Pregnant silence. Speaking again, he raised his voice and did not yell but knocked his clenched fist on the table, "I just don't understand! This is not fair! It's not right! She's worked her whole life for this. You all must have made a mistake."

As he was talking, I was considering the 35,000 other applicants. I was thinking about the thousands of students with nearly perfect grades and SAT/ACT scores. I was considering the hundreds of students who had attained their Gold Award or a black belt in tae kwon do or who had earned their pilot's license or been captain of both the volleyball and tennis teams. In my mind I was thinking about Tech's 23-percent admittance rate and how many students we did not admit—based on the number of available spots in the class—who would clearly do well academically and socially on any campus in the country.

This family was looking to me for a response, but what could I really say in that moment? What would be genuine, accurate, and helpful when I really wanted to say, "I see your point"? I was definitely not going to contest that she was a bright student with excellent grades and impressive involvement outside the classroom. There was nothing *wrong* with her essays or short-answer questions. The recommendations from her teacher and counselor were glowing. Honestly, like most applicants, I could make a case for her to be admitted—and in looking at the notes in her file, one of our admission staff members had done just that. Would she succeed in the classroom? Absolutely. Was she the type of student we would like on campus? Without question. Her school and community involvement, as well as supplemental essays, demonstrated that she would continue to contribute outside the classroom too. Like so many parents, this father was demanding to know exactly why she was denied. He wanted me to point to test scores or grades or the number of clubs she had been part of and say they were "not good enough" or "not high enough."

> When we talk about holistic admission review, we mean there is no numeric formula—there is no *one* thing.

The reality was that numerically we had admitted some students with lower scores or lower grades or less involvement. We had done so based on our undergraduate goals—that is, institutional fit/match, geographic region, curricular interest, or specific academic, personal, or extracurricular background.

When we talk about holistic admission review to prospective families, we mean that there is no numeric formula—there is no *one* thing.

College admission at selective schools is a human process, and as such it is all things human—subjective, imperfect, and more. In the recruitment phase, families find the fact that admission officers are using judgment and context incredibly reassuring. It is ineffably frustrating, however, when a talented student is denied. With this young woman, that was where we sat—and the decision was not going to change.

"You know, she has been offered merit scholarships elsewhere and was admitted to honors colleges at several universities. But you're saying she's not good enough." His daughter winced slightly, and his wife let out an audible sigh as he made his case. At this point, he pulled several acceptance and scholarship letters from other colleges from the manila folder in front of him as evidence. As he pointed to dollar figures and phrases like "invite you" and "congratulations again" and "we hope you'll join," I finally interjected because this was where their focus should be. Right in front of them was hope: letter after letter of choice, opportunity, excitement, support, and belonging. Carefully, I was able to explain that Georgia Tech was no longer an option. Our decisions had been made. Our class was full. Eventually, we moved on to a lengthy but healthy discussion about the other schools and what she hoped to experience and accomplish in college and beyond. Over the course of the next 45 minutes, incredibly, it turned into a warm, productive, and enjoyable conversation that ended with an awkward (but nonetheless appreciated) pseudo group hug.

The truth is we never should have ended up there. Those conversations should have and could have occurred months or even years before at home.

PEOPLE LOVE THEIR KIDS

Unfortunately, each year after decisions are released, admission offices around the country get hundreds of phone calls and emails threatening lawsuits, pledging to write their alma mater out of their will, claiming bias and conspiracy, and informing us that we have ruined their vacation, winter holidays—or life altogether. How does that all feel? Terrible. But thankfully, we know where it comes from.

Regardless of the industry, it is human nature for people to question, examine, shake their head in disapproval, and to express vehement opinions. One of the most public examples of this is in athletics, where coaches are constantly second-guessed by fans about the play they should have called or the player they did not start. We have all turned on the radio or heard this type of Monday-morning chatter at the office or coffee shop: "If I were the coach" or "How could he think that pass was going to work against that defense!" Similar criticism and questioning also exist for accountants, baristas, CEOs, airline gate agents, and chefs. As people, we are perpetually assessing, analyzing, and looking for ways things could or should be improved upon or done differently. Thankfully so—it is what leads to better bridges, more efficient devices, safer car seats, and delicious food.

There is no question that the rising cost of college tuition, increasing debt loads, issues of mental health, and rapidly declining admit rates at our nation's most prestigious institutions are legitimate concerns and contribute to great consternation, speculation, and frustration. The press, politicians, and pundits in community coffee shops and high school bleachers attribute the stress and anxiety surrounding selective college admission to these macro societal issues. The reality, however, is that while these concerns are legitimate, the core of the admission experience is deeply and uniquely personal and relational. If there is one fundamental truth that we have come to appreciate in this work, it is this: people love their kids.

> The admission experience is deeply and uniquely personal and relational.

Even with children of our own and over 40 combined years in college admission and counseling, we are annually reminded of the palpable power of the basic human truth that people love their kids. While obvious, it is also central to fully understanding the college admission experience.

People love their kids. This is why a mother will call pretending to be her daughter in hopes of receiving a password or an admission decision. It is why a father will be in the lobby at 7:30 a.m. after his son was wait-listed the day before. It is why we regularly hear phrases like "*We are taking the SAT next week*" or "*Our first choice is Boston College.*" *People love their kids.* As parents, you have been holding them up since they were born, and even now as young adults, you are figuratively doing just that. When they were little, you could literally pick them up

The truth is the college admission experience is all about family.
Reprinted with the permission of Adam Zyglis.

above your head, spin them around, and hold them close as they smiled and giggled with joy. They trusted you implicitly. They were safe, happy, and excited. As they grew up, you spent countless hours sitting in carpool lines; you finished reading articles waiting for recital practice to finish; you caught up on neighborhood news while waiting for a 30-second leg of a three-hour swim meet; you helped sell cookies or wrapping paper or hams for team, club, or school fundraisers. Hundreds, maybe thousands of miles have been spent visiting family, competing in tournaments, or enjoying a long weekend at the beach or in the mountains. But fundamentally nothing has changed. Sure, they weigh more now, they eat more now, they put more product in their hair, but you are still holding them up—and through all of that change, your desire for their trust, happiness, safety, and excitement has not wavered, because your love is constant.

If you are a student reading this, you need to be reminded of that fact. The admission experience can make your mom or dad go a little wacky at times. Maddening, swirling, repetitive questions about whether you have finished an essay or if you know about certain deadlines or have checked out a specific brochure that they put on your bed last Wednesday may feel like pestering. It can sound like nagging. In reality, it is just 17 years of love in disguise.

EXPERIENCING ADMISSION

There are few experiences short of death, disease, injury or divorce that have as much potential for trauma for American families as the college admissions process. The first great rite of passage for young humans once was killing a wild animal. That was replaced by getting married, or getting a job. These days it is getting into college. —Jay Mathews, *Washington Post*

You could dismiss this as hyperbolic journalism, but the angst surrounding college admission is both palpable and increasing, as the most selective schools around the nation become even more competitive. Fundamentally, much of the anxiety about college admission comes down to the principal concept of economics—supply and demand. Phenomenally talented students from around the world are applying to a similar subset of schools with relatively fixed undergraduate student populations. That you cannot control. What you can control is your approach. You can improve your perspective. You can decide to be true to yourself. The reality is that the college admission experience is just that, an experience, not simply a means to a fixed end, but rather about how your family learns, grows, and embraces this opportunity. Ultimately, the decisions and conversations that your family should be most concerned with are the ones you make in the rooms you go into every day (your living room, your classroom)—the ones you can control—not those made behind closed doors in college admission offices hundreds of miles away.

There are many high-priced educational consultants who will assure you they can predict admission to certain schools. They will claim to polish and package essays or improve test scores to "guarantee" your admittance. This is a misguided use of your time, money, and hope—there is no "Perfect Pathway to Pomona" or "Dartmouth with Distinction" formula to follow. Because this is the case, your goal and vision should not be *which* campus you will walk onto but *how* you will walk through this entire admission experience—together. Most people are focused on "getting in" to a particular school or a very small subset of schools. We hope you will see that the real goal is to gain admission and to stay together as a family. The image of success is not being able to wear a particular school's sweatshirt or place a specific window decal on the back of the car. As you go through the college admission experience, your family's investment should be the same as the one you have always made—to supporting, encouraging, sharing, trusting, and lifting each other up.

> Your goal and vision cannot be *which* campus you will walk onto but *how* you will walk through the admission experience—together.

The college search is an exciting time for students and families. I so wish students could see that they are in the driver's seat when it comes to where they go to college. I realize that they don't always feel like that is the case, but students have the opportunity to <u>choose</u> to which colleges or universities they submit applications. And students then have the opportunity to <u>choose</u> at which college or university they enroll from among their admission offers. —Rachelle Hernandez, Senior Vice Provost for Enrollment Management, the University of Texas–Austin

A COLLEGE SEARCH REDESIGNED

Every summer colleges around the country redesign and reevaluate their "road piece." This is the ubiquitous eight-page brochure that colleges use when traveling to high schools and college fairs throughout the year. You have likely already seen something similar in your mailbox. Here is how it reads:

Page 1: A picture of the football team winning. It is a sunny day, and the school's star player is running triumphantly toward the end zone. The scoreboard either shows (or perhaps has been photoshopped to show) the good guys winning 57–0. Bonus points if you can get a shot with a vanquished opponent on the ground with grass in his facemask or bent over, hands on knees in despair.

Page 2: Three students (typically of different ethnicities) sitting under a tree with a professor. One of the students always has a college-branded shirt, another a worn backpack clearly tossed aside in haste, eager to learn. The professor always strikes an importantly unique balance: youthful energy with sage wisdom, casual professorial fashion without being too unkempt, and always at that perfect distance to connote caring but not creepy. You will notice the students also wear a perfect combination of facial expression and body language that demonstrates they are engaged yet pensive.

Page 3: A student standing on something high—perhaps near a statue or on a mountain or bluff overlooking the ocean at the perfect angle to show the school's logo on her sleeve or hat but also to demonstrate curiosity and limitless possibilities. No brochure is complete without a three-to-four-word, verb-led challenge like *Change Your World*, *Dream Big–Live Bigger*, *Lead the Way*, or *Create the Future*. Countless sticky notes, lunch meetings, and task forces went into establishing that new tag line, and inevitably it will only be moderately adopted around campus and phased out within three years. Rounding out the brochure, one will find cool infographics with admission dates and deadlines, key websites, middle-50-percent ranges of test scores or GPAs, application totals, admit rates, and, of course, rankings.

The rankings an institution chooses to include vary widely. There are the classics: Top 50 Public Universities, Top 100 Colleges in the Nation, and Best Value Schools. However, rankings also allow schools to creatively boast less conventional accolades: "We have the best food selection!" "Our bench-to-student ratio is the lowest in the Midwest!"

There is a ranking for everything.
Each logo printed with the permission of the respective ranking organizations.

"We have the third-highest squirrel-to-student ratio in our conference!" "We are the greenest!" "We play the widest variety of music from the lampposts on the quad!" And the list goes on. More on this in chapter 2.

This year, during Georgia Tech's annual brochure design meeting, I (Rick) suggested we remove the rankings information. Our editor's head tilted slightly to the left and backward as her eyebrows furrowed. Clearly understanding international body language for "What!" I went on to say that we had already removed it from our daily presentation as well.

"But that's the first thing people look for. I see them on campus flipping through to find the rankings." Once she realized that I was not going to respond, she put her palms flat on the table and asked, "OK. Well, if not the rankings, then what do we lead with?"

It is simple really. We need to start with *why* a student should want to come here. *What* makes us different? *Who* are we as a community and an institution? We cannot just market rankings and statistics and expect students and families to connect. We need to combat stereotypes of Georgia Tech (only engineering, urban jungle, students in dark basements wearing lab coats closely examining a beaker with brightly colored liquid) and help students work through the noise of all the schools they are hearing from.

Ultimately that is your challenge as an applicant and as a family. You are going to have to work harder than scanning a list or believing someone who claims they are the sixth best at something. Cutting through the cacophony of college recruitment is not easy because the truth is that we, as colleges, do not do a great job differentiating ourselves in the materials we send, the presentations we give, and the websites we build. After a while, all colleges look the same. Cover up the name of the school on one of the brochures you have lying around. You will find that on the surface you may struggle to see a significant difference between a small, private college in the middle of Ohio and a flagship public university in the Pacific Northwest. As you flip through the pages, both will paint compelling pictures of opportunities to make friends, conduct research, study abroad, work with faculty, receive internship placements, and more.

Colleges will do this on tours too. They intentionally find the most involved students and best ambassadors to talk about all of the amazing research they have done, trips they have taken, and jobs they have lined up. While telling their story, they intersperse equally impressive anecdotes about friends or roommates studying abroad or creating companies—all the while somehow impervious to the 90-degree heat. We have been on tours all over our country in recent years, and these students are amazing—and they are actual humans, not prototypes or conglomerates of a variety of top students. Most adults walk away from campus visits shaking their heads in amazement about their tour guides' talent and brilliance, while silently questioning their relative life accomplishments. (We will provide you tips for maximizing your time on college campuses later in the book but suffice it to say that your consistent and thoughtful questions will be critical.)

If every school seems perfect based on their brochures, websites, and scripted tours, how do you find a college that you will love? Where do you *start*? You start exactly where Tech *restarted* the design process— by looking inward instead of outward and asking questions. You start by redesigning the question to ask, *Why am I going to college?*

YOUR CORNERSTONE QUESTION

In construction, the most important part of the project is not the blueprint or the location or even the style but rather the laying of the cornerstone—also known as the foundation stone. If that piece is not set correctly, the integrity of the entire building is compromised. Everything orients around this integral piece. While it is important to closely research the right location for the building, carefully select the materials, and understand the costs associated with constructing the entire project before you begin, in the end none of that will matter if you do not properly set the cornerstone. Asking the right questions is your cornerstone.

We get it. The list of annoying questions a high school student faces can be long. "So . . . did you finish working on that paper?" "Can I borrow your sweatshirt?" "Are you ready for school?" We are sure you can name a few others that you commonly hear from parents, siblings, coaches, friends, or a boss. But the most frequent, the most repeated, and the most frustrating—and perhaps the only one they might all ask in common—is "Where do you want to go to college?"

While exhausting because of its prevalence, the real problem with the question *where* is not that it is asked with such frequency but rather that it is asked prematurely. On some level, this is logical because much of life in high school points in that direction. Your curriculum or school may be called "college preparatory." Advanced Placement, International Baccalaureate, and opportunities to take university courses all contribute to making college a pervasive part of conversations during your high school years. Even the activities you love and joined for fun become mixed up in the equation: "Keep doing that. It will look great on your college application." "Definitely volunteer too. Colleges want to see that." Because you are surrounded by these types of programs and perspectives, college becomes assumed. It is perceived as inevitable—a foregone conclusion. As a result, far too many students arrive on a campus having never really stepped off the hamster wheel to ask the first question, the more important question, the foundation and cornerstone question—and at its root a family question: *Why are you going to college?*

Why is a lot more complicated and nuanced than *where*. *Where* requires only a one-word response that lacks much thought or deep consideration. "University of X—and done." In contrast, *why* forces introspection and leads you to even more important questions about your college experience.

- Why would you invest this much money in a college education?

- Why are you willing to work hard academically beyond high school to earn a particular degree?

- Why are you going to leave all of your friends and the comfort of the known and move 500 miles away to sleep in a single bed and share a 300-square-foot room?

- Why are you going to study until 3:00 a.m. and eat coffee grounds to stay awake in preparation for a differential equations or British literature exam?

Why is more layered because it leads to big questions like *Who are you?* and *Who do you want to be in the future?* Let's start a little more modestly.

- Who do you hope to meet, connect with, and learn from in college?

- What opportunities do you want this experience to provide in the future?

- How and in what setting do you best learn?

- How far away from home are you willing to go for college?

- What type of people bring out your best?

- How much can you—and should you—pay for this opportunity?

- What is most important to you as you leave high school and look ahead at your next chapter?

Anyone who has been married more than a few years—and certainly anyone who has been married more than once—will say that you have to love yourself, know yourself, and understand yourself before you can possibly commit to a lifetime of loving another person. College is no different. You cannot answer "*Where are you going to college?*" until you first answer "*Why are you going?*" *Why* will lead you to *where*. "I'm looking at this university because they are excellent in the major I want to study," or "because I can build a strong network there," or "because going to school in that city will allow me to continue pursuing my passion for xyz while in college."

> You cannot answer "*Where* are you going to college?" until you first answer "*Why* are you going?"

WHY IS YOUR CORNERSTONE

Fundamentally, asking *why* is your cornerstone. It is your foundation for the entire college experience. *Why* must be asked first, because from it, *where* takes its direction. Asking *why* puts rankings into perspective. It puts the dollars on a return-on-investment chart into perspective. It puts the fact that you are a third-generation Bobcat, Panther, or some other ferocious animal (and you have the picture in the onesie to prove it) into perspective. At the end of the day, *where* should not be answered with "because I look good in those colors" or "because they're national champions" or "because my parents went there" or "because they are number six." Seriously, when was the last time you heard someone run around cheering "We're number six! We're number six!"?

Ask anyone who has been to college, and if they are honest, they can describe a dark, cold day in November of their first year when they sat on their all-too-firm mattress in their residence hall listening to a song that reminded them of high school friends or their hometown. They remember eating mediocre and creatively repurposed food for the eighth straight week or doing laundry at midnight alone or leaving the library bleary-eyed and overcaffeinated. Social media will tell you that college is a never-ending string of sunny days filled with groups of smiling friends going to class outside, but at some point, every first-year student has the same questions rattle around in their head: "Why am I here?" "Did I make the right choice?" "Why does everyone else seem to be doing well, while I am struggling?" Everyone has that day. Everyone has those lonely walks, isolated thoughts, and inevitable doubts. Everyone.

If you skip over *why* and go straight to *where*, your answers will not have a firm foundation. The cornerstone to your entire college search and selection experience will not be properly and securely set. If that is the case, that cold November night will be even more disconcerting. You will not be reassured that you have made the right choice if you never asked or if the answers to *why* are not truly yours. Class sizes, number of squirrels, championship teams, family legacy, and inspiring slogans are not the materials that you want to use as you start to build toward *your* college experience.

We cannot help you diminish the number of people who will inevitably ask you *where*. But we can promise that question will be far less annoying if you have the confidence of knowing *why* certain schools are on your mind or on your college list. *Why* will lead you to *where*. Don't skip a step. Crawl before you walk. Lay that cornerstone first.

 Try This

Here is what we know. The incessant, ubiquitous query "Where do you want to go to college?" will continue. So the next time this is broached by a well-intentioned relative or family friend, redirect the conversation to *why*, and then ask a few questions of your own.

1. **Ask** them *why* they went to college. You will find that friends and family can provide you some questions to add before you begin considering *where*.

2. **Redirect** the conversation. Ask them to look back and consider how they would go about their college experience differently.

3. **Challenge** them to recommend colleges and universities they think would make sense for you, after listening to your reasons for *why* you are going to college.

 Talk About This

1. *Why* do you want to go to college? For parents—why do you want your child to go to college?

2. Which schools are on your list to visit or apply to? Does your *where* still match your *why*? If not, discuss the reasons these schools appear.

3. After reading this chapter, what do you think will be your biggest challenge individually and as a family in the college admission experience?

👍 **CHECK IN** After reading this chapter, are you still on the same page? If you are not all-in together, what do you need to do, discuss, or learn to get there?

CHAPTER 2

Remapping the Admission Landscape

And the people in the houses / All went to the university, /
Where they were put in boxes / And they came out all the same.
"LITTLE BOXES" BY MALVINA REYNOLDS

We have discussed the importance of asking, perhaps for the first time, "*Why* am I going college?" before ever considering *where* that may actually be. We asked you to consider questions about the types of people you want to spend your time with, the experiences you hope to have in a campus community, and the ideal classroom environment that allows you to learn and engage. Lastly, we implored you to put family first—to remain committed to unity, trust, support, and encouragement.

Now that you have reset your foundation for approaching the college experience, you are ready to build around it. What better way to learn how to take logical next steps than a quiz? Do not worry. This will not be graded. There are no prizes for correct responses or penalties for wrong ones, so no Googling answers or asking Alexa or Siri. Pencils ready?

1. Approximately how many colleges and universities are there in the United States (including private, public, community

colleges, two-year schools, four-year universities, technical, arts, comprehensive, etc.)?
☐ 1,000
☐ 6,500
☐ 2,800
☐ 4,600

2. Approximately how many four-year colleges and universities are there in the United States?
☐ 3,000
☐ 460
☐ 2,000
☐ 1,500

3. Of the four-year colleges and universities, how many admit less than one-third of applicants, that is, their admit rate is less than 33 percent?
☐ 550
☐ 100
☐ 425
☐ 1,200

We will provide answers later in the chapter. First, a story.

A few years ago, my family (Rick) went to take holiday pictures in Piedmont Park, Atlanta's equivalent of Central Park. Before I delve into this too far, let me first apologize on behalf of parents everywhere for subjecting kids to holiday pictures. Whether you have been asked to wear "that new shirt" or to "sit casually" on a bench while smiling with your head tilted awkwardly, and certainly if you and 14 others have been dragged to a beach wearing jeans, no shoes, and untucked casual white button-downs, I am truly sorry.

At the time, our daughter (Elizabeth) was three and our son (AJ) was six. Piedmont Park is beautiful, but the geese can be aggressive and Elizabeth was wearing an off-white dress (a terrible decision in hindsight), so my biggest concern was keeping her dry and unscathed. As my wife and the photographer walked briskly to scout out the next location for a picture, AJ took off on a trail in the opposite direction.

After looking for him for about five minutes, we came around a bend to find him six feet up and eight feet out on a magnolia branch.

Andrew "AJ" Clark, age six, Piedmont Park, Atlanta, Georgia.

Wearing khaki pants, a light blue button-down shirt, and a navy sweater vest, he was sitting in a meditational pose: legs crossed, eyes gently closed, fingers touching, and his arms overlapping at the wrists. I saw his left eye open ever so slightly, and he said in the deepest voice a six-year-old can muster, "Look beyond what you see!" My first thought was, "Wow. This kid is kind of weird," which was followed by, "and yet he may also be a prophet, which would be interesting and potentially lucrative."

As any scholar of film will know, he was referencing one of the real gems of American movie history, *The Lion King 1½*. In the scene, Rafiki, the wise old baboon, challenges Timon to look beyond what he sees in order to find Hakuna Matata: a life of no worries. While we cannot promise you that exactly, there is still much to learn from this sage advice.

LOOK BEYOND WHAT YOU SEE

It is tougher than you would think as you consider colleges, but it's absolutely critical to look beyond what you see.

- More than 270 American universities with undergraduate populations over 20,000 (IPEDS Data Retrieval Center 2016–2017)

- More than 1,500 colleges with undergraduate populations under 1,000 (IPEDS Data Retrieval Center 2016–2017)

- Approximately 980 public community colleges (Statista 2018)

- Average admit rate of Big 10 (a.k.a. Big 14): 55 percent (Grove 2018)

- Median admit rate of Southeastern Conference (SEC): 67.5 percent (IPEDS Data Retrieval Center 2016–2017)

- Median admit rate of PAC 12: 74 percent (IPEDS Data Retrieval Center 2016–2017)

- Number of American students attending college outside the United States: 46,500 (Belyavina, Li, and Bhandari 2013)

- Over 100 historically black colleges and universities (IPEDS Data Retrieval Center 2016–2017)

- Over 400 not-for-profit colleges and universities in California (IPEDS Data Retrieval Center 2016–2017)

- Over 50 colleges in Arkansas (IPEDS Data Retrieval Center 2016–2017)

- Nearly 74,000 first-year students in SEC schools (IPEDS Data Retrieval Center 2016–2017)

- Over 1,400 colleges with undergraduate populations between 1,000 and 5,000 (IPEDS Data Retrieval Center 2016–2017)

- Nearly 300 US colleges and universities that start with the letter *B* (IPEDS Data Retrieval Center 2016–2017)

- Approximately 61,000 total undergraduates in the eight Ivy League schools (IPEDS Data Retrieval Center 2016–2017)

- Over 53,000 undergraduates attending Texas A&M–College Station (IPEDS Data Retrieval Center 2016–2017)

- Nearly 100,000 undergraduates attending the Texas A&M system schools (IPEDS Data Retrieval Center 2016–2017)

The prospect of a college education should be filled with possibility, hope, and joy—and so should the experience to get there. Attitude is everything, so start by internalizing that it really, truly is all going to work out. The great strength of our higher education system is its incredible diversity. As you embark on this journey, suspend your preconceived notions about what "the right" school is and open your mind to the countless number of incredible options out there for your student. You'll be amazed at the possibilities, and you'll discover some hope and joy along the way. —Jenny Rickard, President and CEO, The Common Application

————

Back to our quiz. Ready for a few answers?

1. **Question:** How many colleges and universities are there in the United States (including private, public, community colleges, two-year schools, four-year universities, technical, comprehensive, etc.)?

   Answer: about 4,600 (US Department of Education 2018)

2. **Question**: How many four-year colleges and universities are there in the United States?

   Answer: about 3,000 (US Department of Education 2018)

3. **Question:** How many four-year colleges in the country admit less than one-third of applicants, that is, their admit rate is less than 33 percent (and they would be considered "selective" or "highly selective")?

   Answer: about 100 (*U.S. News and World Report* 2018)

Having asked these exact questions all over the country during presentations and panels, we are guessing you underestimated your answers to numbers 1 and 2 and overestimated your response to number 3. You may also find it surprising to know that only around 50 colleges offer admission to less than 25 percent of applicants (*U.S. News and World Report* 2018). In fact, the average acceptance rate at four-year schools has consistently remained above 64 percent (Clinedinst and Patel 2018). Each summer, the National Association for College Admission Counseling (NACAC) publishes its College Openings Update list. In most years, well over 500 schools are still accepting applications for students in the final months before the new academic year begins (NACAC College Openings Update 2018).

What does this mean for you? It means that getting into most colleges and universities around our country is not the real challenge for students who are doing well in high school. Instead it underscores the fact that there are hundreds of academically excellent and financially affordable colleges looking to admit and enroll talented students who will not only succeed inside the classroom but also contribute in a meaningful and influential way within the campus community. In his role as executive director for educational content and policy at NA-CAC, David Hawkins works alongside hundreds of admission and counseling professionals each year. He offers sage advice: "When counselors and admission officers talk to you about 'finding the right *fit*,' this is what they're talking about. Getting into college is not an end unto itself; it's not a 'skins game' of seeing how many colleges you can get accepted to. It's about taking your first steps as an adult, and laying the foundation for the rest of your life. In that light, it doesn't make sense to choose colleges on any basis *other* than what's right for you."

> Hundreds of academically excellent and affordable colleges are looking to admit and enroll talented students.

Later in the book, we will discuss holistic admission and how admission decisions are made, but for now you need to understand these statistics and this fact: most schools are simply *looking to admit and enroll* good students.

Write down the first five colleges that come to your mind.

- What do they have in common?

- Are the majority of them in the same geographic area?

- Are they all private schools or public universities?

- How did you hear about them?

- Do most oddly start with the letter B or play sports in the same athletic conference?

Spend some time comparing your list to those of other family members, and ask friends or classmates to do this exercise.

- Do you find a lot of overlap on your list compared with that of the people you know and spend time with?

- What do your responses tell you about the way you currently think about college?

THE VALUE OF PERSPECTIVE

Too many students and families have a myopic or simply dated view of the higher education landscape. Our goal throughout this book is to remind you of just how vast it really is, to demonstrate that your choices are extensive, and then to help you determine which of those colleges are good matches for you.

Think about your own state. How many colleges can you name? The next time you are on a road trip, keep an eye on the exit signs for universities. They are everywhere: colleges bearing the names of cheese (Colby College, American University), universities designed by or honoring former presidents (George Washington University, Lincoln University, University of Virginia), schools with multiple directions in the same word (Northwestern University, Nova Southeastern University). Walk the halls of your high school during the fall, and you will likely see posters from colleges all over the country and the world.

Maintaining an open mind and looking beyond what you see is your job in the college search and admission experience. Regardless of where you live, this can be difficult. Students from your high school often go to many of the same colleges after they graduate. You see the same schools playing sports on TV and the same window decals on the backs of cars in the parking lot. Naturally, your frame of reference is limited.

The good news is that colleges will help keep your perspective broad if you will let them. They make it incredibly easy to remember just how many choices you have by delivering themselves to your home. Remember those recruitment brochures from chapter 1? Generally, beginning in your sophomore year and then really ramping up as a junior, these start appearing in your mailbox (and email inbox).

COLLEGE SEARCH: A TWO-WAY STREET

The college admission process is a two-way street. That's right. You are not the only one searching for a good college match. Universities are doing this too. In fact, there is an entire industry around "search"—because it is big business.

Here is how this works. When you register for standardized tests, including the PSAT, SAT, ACT, TOEFL, SAT Subject Tests, and AP Tests, there is an option for you to check a box indicating your willingness to share your information with universities.

> Universities are searching for a good college match too—and it is big business.

Colleges and universities contract with the College Board or ACT to access databases and purchase names and contact information. This allows them to build what are known as "search campaigns" to identify high school students who seem to be good matches. They are able to segment their search by an incredible number of factors.

A CASE STUDY

"Example College" is a private school of 6,500 students located in the Northeast. Recently, they were thrilled to receive a new $20 million gift to enhance the Chemistry Department. The president has announced plans to build a new facility and endow a chair position. The donor also specified that she would like to see a 25 percent increase in females majoring in chemistry over the next five years.

Translation: For the vice president of enrollment management or dean/director of admission, bolstering enrollment and gender equity in the chemistry department has just become an institutional priority, or IP. (Later in the book, we will discuss how IPs affect admission decisions, but they also strongly influence recruitment budgets, travel, programming, communications efforts, and search buys.)

To begin to work toward this specific enrollment goal, Example College will first determine the number of prospects they already have in their customer relationship management system (CRM) (see figure on page 26). This is a traditional enrollment funnel. As you will notice, it begins broadly with "prospects" and then slowly filters down through the stages of admission (applicant, admit, confirmed, enrollee).

At this point, admission leaders analyze the academic and demographic (geographic, gender, ethnic, etc.) profile of their current students

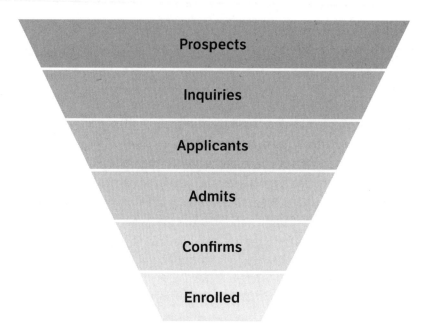

Example of the traditional enrollment funnel.

and then devise a search strategy to help them meet this new target. After they determine how many additional female students they will need to enroll in chemistry each year, they are ready to log in to the College Board and ACT databases to purchase student names.

In order to narrow the funnel, step by step, schools select criteria for the type of students they want to communicate with and encourage to apply. This is known as a "search purchase." A sound search strategy essentially marries a school's IPs with their recruitment budget.

Note: Each student name purchased costs $0.42 from both ACT and College Board. All calculations below are calculated using that price point.

Here is how Example College's "buy" would go as they refine their purchase:

Contact Information: including mailing address, cell numbers, and email (colleges can select either or both, assuming the student has provided each)—2 million names, or $840,000

Graduation Year: sophomores, juniors, seniors—1,600,000 names, or $672,000

Major: chemistry—200,000 names, or $84,000

Geography: all New England and Middle Atlantic states (in this section you can also buy according to zip code, radius from a city, individual state, nation, county, etc.; currently, you cannot buy based solely on high school)—60,000 names, or $25,200

Gender: female—25,000 names, or $10,500

Ethnicity: all—25,000 names, or $10,500

High School GPA: B+ or above (self-reported by the student and identified on a scale of A–D including plus and minus)—18,000 names, or $7,560

Test Scores: This is a little more complicated. SAT and PSAT scores are released in increments of 50. If the current SAT average of Example College students is 1320, they will likely buy slightly lower (especially when they are purchasing names of sophomores and juniors, because statistics demonstrate that those scores will increase on subsequent administrations of the tests, and they want to start recruiting them early). Example College's SAT/PSAT: 1250+ SAT (or they could use a range with a floor and ceiling,* i.e., 1250–1400) ACT: 26+ (or 26–30)—15,000 names, or $6,300

After entering their search criteria, Example College would ultimately pay $6,300 for those 15,000 names of potential future female chemistry majors from the Northeast to meet this new goal. There was a time when a university would need to wait weeks to receive these data. That delay was gradually reduced to days, and now the time between submitting and paying for a search purchase and the actionable receipt of being able to call, email, or send hard-copy mail to students is essentially immediate.

Because there are multiple test administrations every year, most schools will purchase and receive names after either each exam or each

---

*Buying names of students with no upper limit versus a range is a philosophical decision. Schools need to ask themselves whether they are in a market position to compete for students at the very highest score bands. It can also be a purely monetary decision based on overall search budget.

season of exams (summer, fall, winter, spring). They also have the option to submit a recurring search or standing order that ensures they receive new names of qualifying students once they are available from ACT or College Board. In other words, Example College will be investing additional money later that year and in the years to come in order to achieve their five-year target. Keep in mind that, at this point, Example College has yet to pay to produce marketing materials geared toward chemistry majors. They will still need to allot additional budget resources toward the postage necessary to mail out their glossy brochures of happy students wearing lab goggles next to caring professors in impressive facilities. As you can see, the costs add up quickly.

Example College is fictitious, but the search industry is very real. Our scenario presumes that, unlike hundreds of schools nationally, Example College is not outsourcing their search purchase strategy or brand management to an outside firm. Quotes for that kind of work normally start around $50,000, and annual investments reaching into the hundreds of thousands of dollars are commonplace in higher education. To provide you some additional perspective on the scope of the search industry, for many years Ed Gillis (the former vice president of enrollment at the University of Miami) published a search summary report in conjunction with the Harvard Summer Institute on Admission. College and university names were redacted and some data were aggregated, but it outlined the number of student names participating schools were buying. The average number of unique names contacted by colleges was around 150,000, or $63,000 at $0.42 each. The top of the range was over 500,000 (or $210,000). The odds are that there were schools not participating in this survey who were, and likely still are, conducting searches at well over that mark. We have not even delved into the complexity, scope, and cost of purchasing and mailing information to the ever-growing international market of students who are considering college in the United States. In recent years, well over one million students from abroad have come to the United States to pursue their education (Fast Facts 2018).

Adding to the equation and magnitude of the financial investment in college recruitment is that searches extend well beyond standardized testing. Until July 2018, when they were acquired by ACT, the National Research Center for College and University Admissions (NRCCUA) was

> Searches extend well beyond standardized testing.

an educational data science and research organization that administered surveys to high school students. Many colleges also bought names from NRCCUA to procure contact information for younger students—those who either did not take or had not yet taken standardized testing. After spending millions of dollars to purchase NRCCUA, ACT will administer those surveys to develop and sell lists of names.

We told you search was big business.

TAKEAWAY LESSONS

The case of Example College should help you understand where all of those brochures are coming from and how schools are searching for you. While it may be interesting (or moderately disconcerting) to understand the amount of money and effort colleges are spending to find you, the real lesson is that you should be emulating their approach to college search.

1. *Think like a dean.* Look again at the admission funnel. Any dean or director of admission would love to only buy the exact number of "enrollees" for their class each year. If they could determine exactly who would be interested in the college, apply, be eligible for admission, be able to pay tuition, choose to attend, succeed on campus, graduate on time, and give back to the school as alumni, they could literally save tens (sometimes hundreds) of thousands of dollars. But that is not how it works. They start with casting a wide net. They start by thinking about their goals and entering into conversations with students by telling them about their programs, inviting them to visit campus, connecting them with current students, staff, and faculty, and so on. They do not begin with *exactly* who will make up their class but instead with the type of students they are trying to recruit. As a sophomore and junior in high school, you should be doing the same thing. The odds are that your list is too narrow right now. This means you are likely starting too far down in your own admission search funnel. We want to challenge you to start broad—start at the top. You will learn how to do this in chapter 4.

2. *Check that box.* When you take standardized tests (including the PSAT, Pre-ACT, SAT, ACT, etc.) or when a survey is distributed in your

high school for the purposes of college recruitment, we recommend that you opt in. Yes, this means you will be inundated with mail and email that you will need to manage. However, as we have established, one of the biggest problems students and families face is a narrow perspective—overlooking the vast landscape and believing inaccurately that options are limited. Providing your contact information protects against that. Colleges are checking boxes as they craft their search purchases and strategy. While this is your choice, we are encouraging you to do the same. You paid to take the test. Receiving recruitment information is a benefit you receive for that registration fee. Check that box.

3. *Segment your search.* When colleges receive their search order, they then determine the appropriate communication flow based on the student's profile. For instance, if Example College knows that the most common prototype of a chemistry student on their campus is a female from New Jersey with a 1300–1400 SAT, they will likely choose not to mail extensively to that demographic. Instead, they will push those names into an email-only campaign. Conversely, if they know it is tougher to enroll students from Massachusetts, they may segment that population for a more consistent or individualized campaign. You should be doing the exact same thing. We recommend that once these brochures start showing up, you put three boxes in your room or somewhere in your house. First, a box labeled "considering": this does not mean that you plan to definitely apply or visit but simply that someone in the family believes this school aligns with your answers from chapter 1 about *why* you are going to college. It is potentially a good match. Second, a box labeled "for a friend": colleges will be the first to tell you that search is imperfect. While they need to buy names to expand their applicant pool and meet institutional priorities, many of their inquiries (next level down on the funnel) do not come as a result of their search purchase. They come from people who visit campus or those who complete interest forms online and many times because they were referred by alumni, neighbors, or friends. When you receive information from a school that does not fit with your answers to *why* you are going to college, think about who you know that may be interested and pass these along. Lastly, a box labeled "recycle": do not be lazy. Do not throw all of these lovely marketing materials in the trash. Let's work together to save the world one college brochure at a time!

In fact, if you take nothing else away from this section, it is this: recycle.

You will also be getting a lot of email. A lot. We strongly recommend you create an email address just for your college search that is separate from your personal account. Whether you decide to provide shared access to all family members is an individual decision. You will want to create similar subfolders in that account—consider, visit, apply—and ultimately folders for each individual college. The good news about email is you will be able to forward to a friend, unsubscribe, or mark as junk. It may be dull, but we strongly recommend that you choose a generic email address: in other words, firstname.lastname2021@gmail.com or something to that effect. We have both had to send emails to addresses like inittowinit@hotmail.com, studdawg@gmail.com, and so on. Many colleges will create an internal list at the end of the year of the most odd or inappropriate emails in their applicant pool. You do not want to be on that list. Recycle, and do not be on that list. Promise us those two things.

4. *Work the funnel.* If you receive mail or email from a school you are interested in hearing more from, you need to take action. Often the materials you receive in the mail include physical tear-offs to send back or a QR code to respond to or a URL to follow. When you do this, colleges will update your record to reflect that interest. Demonstrating your interest in these ways frequently means you will be invited to programs, sent more specific details about your interests, and asked to engage with the campus community. You are now moving down the funnel from prospect to inquiry. Work the funnel.

> **Thousands of schools are spending tens of thousands of dollars to recruit you.**

We hope that you now have a bigger perspective on the landscape of higher education in our nation: thousands of schools spending tens of thousands of dollars to recruit you. In fact, according to a survey of colleges produced by the enrollment consulting firm Ruffalo Noel Levitz (2018), the median cost for a four-year private institution to recruit a student in 2017 was $2,357.

Ultimately, your family's job is to keep that perspective. Do your job! You have lots of options and choices. Do not limit yourself. Do not start at the bottom of the funnel.

🔆 *Try This*

Pick up a copy of the illustrated book *Zoom* by Istvan Banyai. Keep this with you as you go through your college search experience. Here is why: On the first page of the book, you see a picture of a bunch of red triangles. The next page zooms out to show that those triangles are actually a rooster who is being watched through a window by two children. Zooming back again on the next page, you see that the children are actually toys in a set being played with by a little girl. Page after page, we zoom out from the original scene. By the end, the entire scene turns out to be a cover of a magazine being read on a cruise that is actually an ad on a side of a bus. Too many students and families get stuck on page 1 of *Zoom* (metaphorically). Their list of ten colleges does not change. Effectively, they are seeing only the same small red triangles. We are encouraging you to pull back and adjust your lens. A college search done well—a college search done as a family—means you cross schools off, add new ones, and continually modify, compare, revisit, and revise. Later in the book, we will provide you tools for allocating time and the necessary questions to ask to ensure you are communicating effectively. For now we are simply urging you to see the broader landscape, to zoom back, to look beyond what you see. Choices. Many, many choices. Your job is not to lose sight of that.

🔆 *Try This (Extra Credit)*

Our friend Jeff Kurtzman, the director of college counseling at the McCallie School, has his entire junior class listen to the song "Little Boxes." (Written and composed by Malvina Reynolds, it was popularized by Pete Seeger, although we are partial to the version by Walk Off the Earth.) This song, originally a political satire about suburbia, is a creative way to frame the college search and admission experience. We encourage you to listen to this (somewhat campy) song together and discuss how it may be helpful as you go through your college admission experience.

🗨 Talk About This

1. What do you think will be the biggest challenge or obstacle to keeping an open mind as you go through the college search and application experience? Why?

2. List five factors in your family/school/community experience that could contribute to a narrow approach to finding colleges.

3. After reading this chapter, what are you most excited about in the college search and application experience? Why?

4. Based on what you have read so far, how does the list of colleges you are interested in visiting or applying to change? Write down one or two reasons each school you are considering is of interest.

👍 **CHECK IN** After reading this chapter, are you still on the same page? If you are not all-in together, what do you need to do, discuss, or learn to get there?

CHAPTER 3

Wedges of College Admission

Let's stay together / Lovin' you whether /
Times are good or bad, happy or sad.
"LET'S STAY TOGETHER" BY AL GREEN

If your family has ever sold a house, you know how all-consuming it can be. First, you have to prepare to sell by decluttering inside, touching up outside, and buying odd, decorative items for show, such as doilies and cookie-scented candles. Once on the market, you are at the mercy of potential buyers. When your real estate agent alerts you that you have a "showing," it sets off a furious succession of wiping, cleaning, throwing a few scattered items into a box, and leaving the house to take refuge in sometimes random locations.

The buying side can be worse. After downloading every possible real estate app—Zillow, Redfin, Trulia, Falsia (and at least one more for good measure)—you set parameters for the desired number of bedrooms, bathrooms, location, price, and so on. Then the notifications start coming—or they don't. Either way it is maddening. If your family is moving locally, every trip to the grocery store becomes a detour "just to see if a new home has popped up on the market." It is easy to become manic about getting in to see houses before other potential buyers. Even the most normal people can find themselves cruising slowly through neighborhoods, while eight-year-olds on bikes return curious and suspicious looks.

The conversation at every meal is about particular houses, pricing, or speculation about what you should do or should have done or what might happen next week. Everyone in the family (even those who do not live with you or even visit often) seems to have an opinion or a suggestion.

WE'RE MOVING!

There are a lot of parallels between home buying and college admission. You are constantly receiving shiny brochures advertising amazing "properties" that you simply must see! They tout all their amenities and provide testimonials that encourage you to dream about what life would be like living there. So you tour colleges and create pros-and-cons lists about size, price, location, and other factors. You inevitably find conflicting or incomplete information online, just like with the real estate apps and websites. Everyone from coaches to aunts to baristas are asking you questions and expressing their opinions about the place you should choose, which schools are overpriced, and those that are unwarranted in their popularity. It is an uncertain and protracted timeline. And let's face it: as humans we just hate the waiting.

> The college admission experience can be exhausting, confusing, and filled with tension.

Every year we see that, for many students and families, the college admission experience, like the home-buying and home-selling process, is exhausting, confusing, and filled with tension. In this chapter, we identify the primary wedges that divide families and provide you with tools and approaches to help keep you on the same page.

WEDGE #1: TIME

If you are not intentional about when you have conversations about searching for, applying to, and ultimately deciding on a college, the subject can bleed into almost any discussion. Parents' non sequiturs are the first sign of this problem: "Will you please put the ketchup back in the fridge, and be sure to ask Mrs. Thomas to write that recommendation for you." "Remember, it's your grandma's birthday, so let's call her later. And how about that letter from UConn?"

Left unchecked, these queries and reminders feel like relentless Zillow notifications to students because they pop up incessantly—after practice, on the way home from school, during breakfast, through the bathroom door, or while sitting on the porch trying to relax. Students begin to feel like every time they come downstairs for a meal, the "college talk" begins. Parents feel like their intelligent offspring has somehow lost the ability to string consecutive words together or convey ideas in multisyllabic words. More importantly, these situations create unnecessary tension and division. Beware of the creep (verb, not noun) of college conversations!

☑️ QUICK QUIZ

Parents: Are you bringing up various college options, deadlines, or test dates at unnatural times with unchecked repetition throughout the week?

Students: Do you frequently answer your parents' sequential questions about college with "Good," "Okay," "No," "Huh?" Do you pretend like your phone is ringing and head for the car when Mom asks, "Have you taken that practice SAT online yet?"

If the answer to any of these questions is *yes*, we strongly encourage the implementation of a consolidated time each week when college is on the proverbial—and perhaps literal—table.

We recommend that you identify a consistent, mutually agreed-upon hour a week beginning in the spring of junior year. Occasionally, this may need to be closer to two hours at points in senior year. Perhaps you set aside Sunday afternoons or Thursday nights. If you will isolate this time (and cancel it in weeks you do not need to meet), you will help bolster family unity and ensure that your relationship does not unnecessarily narrow to a focus solely on college.

House Rules

Parents: You *get to bring* brochures you have noticed in the mail. This is *your time* to say, "Hey, look, honey, the leaves are turning in Ohio. Isn't it pretty?" You *get to ask*, "Have you written your supplemental essays for SMU?" Or "Do you still want to take that trip to California to look at schools in November?" This is your time for "Did you get your ACT results back?" It's all fair game.

You *don't get to bring* outdated stereotypes of colleges and universities based on your experiences 20 or 30 years ago. You *don't get to* fold your arms or have knee-jerk reactions. This is a family conversation. Resist the temptation to discuss other students or families and their college search or application experience (and by all means do not compare your children to each other).

Students: You *get to bring* ideas about colleges you are interested in and permission slips for your parents to sign to go on a school-sponsored college trip. This is *your time* to ask for another set of eyes on an essay or to broach the fact that you are planning to apply to the rival university of your mom's alma mater. It is also your time to talk about why you may no longer be interested in a specific major, location, school, or anything else.

You *don't get to bring* your cell phone or really crunchy snacks. You *don't get* to look at your shoes more than three times or for beyond six seconds. Come ready to fully engage in the conversation. Use intonation. Do not use sarcasm. Have some questions of your own ready about what you need. Come to this time the way you show up to an athletic practice—ready to put in the work and improve individually and as a team. Same thing here. One time a week—for an hour or two. That's 1 percent of your entire week. You got this!

The reason your parents are bringing up college, asking you questions, and expressing their opinions is partly because they are not convinced you are on it. If you answer their questions, show you have a plan, and demonstrate that you are making progress on setting up campus visits or completing applications and paying attention to deadlines, you will dramatically diminish the seemingly incessant nagging. In truth, it is not really nagging at all. Instead, it is simply them doing what they have always done—loving you by trying to look out for you. Think about it—all of these questions are really just love in disguise. The time your parents make, the questions they ask, their desire to see things taken care of—these are absolutely grounded in deep affection. They know you are going to head off to college soon. There is some fear in that—and a lot of excitement. Every now and then they cannot believe you are taking AP Biology or standing at over six feet tall. Somehow carpool lines and training wheels do not seem like that long ago. Fear, excitement, love—these all warrant you being fully engaged, so meet their love halfway and err on the side of too much information. Answer their questions, look them in the eye, put down your phone, and for bonus points, start and end the time with a hug. Yes, we are serious.

The good news is that, as a senior, the two-hour rule holds true when you are working on your applications too. You will find that if you devote that time consistently (not just the last three hours before the deadline!) for six or seven weeks, you can absolutely do a great job on your applications. In truth, your essays will be better by drafting and then revisiting them in multiple sittings. Like many important things in life, there is a lot to be said for letting something sit for a week and then coming back with fresh eyes, some sleep, and a new perspective. In fact, do yourself and your parents a favor, and start this all in the summer before senior year when you are not juggling as many balls.

> **Let your application sit for a week and then come back with fresh eyes.**

WEDGE #2: COMMUNICATION

One of the main issues with home buying and selling is how public it becomes—suddenly you are exposed. Everyone can see pictures, prices, and statistics about square footage or the number of bathrooms on flyers, apps, or websites. Neighbors chat in front yards and speculate about why someone is moving, when the house will sell, who might move in, and if it is over- or underpriced.

Too often we see the same type of unnecessary, unhealthy, and unbridled noise occur in the admission experience because families share too much publicly. For students and parents, we strongly encourage you to limit what you broadcast in conversation and post on social media. Volunteering where you are applying or your first-choice college opens you up to questions later from teachers, relatives, friends, and friends of friends about admission decisions and personal considerations regarding your ultimate college choice.

Keep It Private

Parents: You have the ability to reduce the speculation and consternation surrounding college admission in your community by refraining from sharing stories at athletic games, cocktail parties, or online about where your son or daughter is admitted, denied, offered scholarships. The college admission experience can be a roller coaster because you love your kid. You want the best for them. You know that they are going to leave home soon. You see the big tuition bills coming. You are going to experience a variety of emotions along the way, and it is understandable to want to share those worries, hopes, frustrations, or celebrations with your wider network. Being disciplined to keep these considerations and deliberations private has incredible potential to build trust and create strong bonds in your family during what should be a very personal time. We know this is not easy, but it will make the celebrations of admission or scholarships sweeter when they come.

We would also challenge you not to ask other parents about their family's college admission search. Not only is it really none of your business, but likely the information shared is exaggerated or inaccurate. Typically, it only makes you—and by extension your family—more anxious. Instead of interrogating other parents in the middle of the experience, we encourage you to talk to parents who have been through this before. They have tremendous perspective to share and encouragement to provide. (We also guarantee you that none of them will say they wish they had made their college admission experience more public.)

Students: Consider holding this experience a little closer to your vest (or sweater or shirt for nonvest wearers) and only let a small subset of trusted people know the details of your college search. Build a "College Support Team." This group would include your parents, a classmate or two, your counselor, and a teacher. These are the people that you use as your sounding board. Ask them to review your answers to

"Why are you going to college?" and honestly critique or challenge your rationale. These are the opinions and voices you trust to weigh in when you are building your college list. Talk to them after you visit colleges; consult with them about your essay topic; count on them to read and improve your writing with their suggestions; and request that they help you prepare for your interviews.

Assembling and counting on this group is not just an opportunity to learn more about yourself through their feedback but also to deepen these relationships, as they invest in you, keep you accountable, and encourage you along the way. When you are deferred, denied, or waitlisted by a college, you have a group ready to console or empathize and also to encourage you and provide that priceless perspective that you will need. In contrast, when you are admitted or receive a great financial aid package, this group will be thrilled to come around to both celebrate and validate all you have done to earn those opportunities.

Watch Your Pronouns

Setting aside time to discuss college and keeping your discussions relatively private will help your family significantly. The other primary issue with communication is that parents, in their desire to help and support, often overreach and try to drive the entire search and application experience. When this happens, students get frustrated and/or shut down.

Parents: We have already established that you love your kids—but *you are not them.* Every year admission offices receive calls like this: "*We* were deferred from your college. I know that you've received *our* transcript and supplement (because I made him give me his log-in info), and I see from your website that you don't use an interview or additional letters of recommendation in the process, but I'm going to have two of my business associates email on his behalf anyway." Admission staff often see students slump down in their chairs at information sessions (and even a few get up and walk out) when Dad launches into question number seven or watch a student fade to the back of the tour when Mom grills the tour guide incessantly.

> ☑️ **THE PARENTAL PRONOUN TEST**
>
> - *If* you've recently said, "We are taking the SAT next weekend," *then* you might be overly involved.
>
> - *If* you said to a friend in the bleachers last week, "Our first choice is Columbia," *then* you might need to go for a walk.
>
> - *If*, as your daughter was leaving for school the other day, you said, "Let's ace that calculus exam!" *then* you might need to take a deep breath and rethink your approach.

Our hope is that you will shift your stance from a "we" that can be overreaching and at times divisive to one that is helpful in maintaining unity, such as the following:

We can discuss financing college at the outset.

We can limit talk about college to one day a week.

We can challenge each other to think beyond reputation, assumptions, or preconceived notions.

We can tour a range of colleges and each form different impressions.

We can be aware of expectations and talk openly about these as a family.

We can resist the temptation to make comparisons to siblings, relatives, or friends.

We can laugh, cry, celebrate, and be disappointed—sometimes simultaneously.

We can realize that change is inevitable and full of potential.

We can listen attentively to others and ourselves.

We can be authentic and not attempt to "game" the admission experience.

We can accept that a college does not define a person.

We can acknowledge that while we each have our own story, our stories are wonderfully and undeniably intertwined.

Matthew Hyde, dean of admission at Lafayette College, has thoughtfully shepherded thousands of families through this journey and makes these observations about how "we" can all be in this together while also allowing students to shine:

The college search experience, when well-informed and good-intentioned, creates an awesome opportunity for young people to gain agency over their narrative. These college hopefuls can (and should) begin to get comfortable penning their own story, and owning the opportunity (arguably obligation) to take charge of their narrative. If not yet co-authoring their own story, this rite of passage moment presents excellent footing for college applicants to begin to do so—honoring those who have raised and cared for them, but confidently taking charge of outlining the chapters to come. Cutting out those who know them best is a bad idea on an applicant's part, but refusing to allow applicants to take charge is equally bad. The "royal we," when appropriately inserted, reflects a nicely balanced evolutionary moment and the passing of the narrative-writing "pen."

In his 2018 *Washington Post* article, "The Compelling Case for Being an 'Intentionally Lazy' Parent," Scott Lutostanski discusses executive function skills, which include organization, time management, and planning. He asserts that parents need to be intentional and disciplined about empowering their kids to grow and develop in these areas. Searching for, visiting, applying to, being accepted to, being disappointed by, and ultimately deciding on a college are all opportunities to help your student augment these invaluable skills.

The communication wedge is real but avoidable.

Periodically checking your pronouns is one of the easiest ways to ensure you are avoiding the communication wedge. It will also help you ask questions about your student's college essays and make helpful edits or suggestions—rather than be tempted to rewrite the essay with words like "lugubrious" or "obsequious." The communication wedge is real but avoidable. In a short year or two, *they* will be on a college campus. *They* will need to be able to advocate and navigate for themselves. Watching your pronouns allows you to step back without stepping away.

Students: Go find some pictures of your family from points in your life. Maybe those are hanging on your wall or piled in a drawer or carefully assembled in an album on your living room shelves. More likely they are downloaded to random folders on a parent's laptop. Regardless, check out the smiles and locations in each photo. Think back over all the time your parents have dedicated to you, all the love they have shown you, the work done for your well-being, and the sacrifices they have made for you. The number of carpool lines they endured, the recitals and games they watched and drove to, the lunches packed or dinners prepared.

Read the "Parental Pronoun Test." It was hard for them. This is *all* hard for them. They love you so deeply that their life (and sometimes their words) has become interwoven with yours. Take some time this week (and ideally at some point during each of your weekly meetings) to say two things to them: (1) Thank you. (2) I love you. Trust us—they need to hear it. (1) Thank you. (2) I love you. If you can keep doing that at least once a week until you head off to college (ideally, keep doing it forever), there is no wedge that can drive you apart. (Don't worry, we will remind you to do this at the end of the book.)

I tell my students to take ownership over the college admission process. While that partly means taking responsibility for all moving parts of the process, it really means taking ownership over their own voice. Parents, friends, and family members usually have the best intentions about giving college admission and selection advice, but the student needs to take inventory about what drives them. Ultimately, compromise and agreement is the goal but students need to know they've had an opportunity to be the driving force in *their* future plans.
—Brandi Smith, School Counselor, Marietta High School, Georgia

---

WEDGE #3: MONEY

When you are buying a house, price is often the first filter you apply to your search. *What can we afford?* Location, size, number of bathrooms, and considerations like brick versus siding matter, but typically cost is your first narrowing factor. Money becomes a wedge in the college search and selection experience when parents determine a price range with limited (and even inaccurate) information and without having honest conversations early in the search.

Understanding Costs

Colleges and universities that receive federal funding must publish their school's *total cost of attendance* (COA), which includes not only tuition, room and board, but also averages for fees, books, supplies, transportation, and personal expenses. A 2018 report by the National Center for Education Statistics revealed that families often overestimate what they will ultimately pay to attend a particular school (Velez and Horn 2018). One of the primary reasons is that simply looking at tuition, room, and board does not tell the whole picture: "Published college sticker prices, which few students pay, and media attention to high-cost private colleges and universities may contribute to students' and families' common misapprehensions about the price of attendance."

Example

The University of North Carolina–Chapel Hill (for in-state students) costs just over $24,000 annually (University of North Carolina–Chapel Hill n.d.). Duke University costs nearly $73,000 annually (Duke University n.d.).

Separated by only a few miles and shades of blue, these two institutions both have incredible reputations for enrolling and graduating students who go on to achieve tremendous success. However, upon seeing these costs and making a direct comparison, a family may rule out Duke as being out of their price range. (Granted, in some cases, basketball allegiance may also be a factor.) Understanding college costs is more nuanced than evaluating home prices (or basketball teams for that matter). At Duke, due to their ability to meet a family's demonstrated financial need, fewer than half of their students pay the full published cost.

Net Price

John Leach, assistant vice provost for enrollment and director of financial aid at Emory University, implores families to use the Net Price Calculator, which the US Department of Education requires each school to make available on their institution's financial aid website. The *net price* is the amount you can expect to pay after receiving financial aid. "Use those net price calculators *as soon as you start thinking about college*," Leach advises. He explains that by entering basic information into this resource, you will be able to get a "very good sense" of what families at that school who have similar savings, earnings, assets, and financial situations to yours have paid in recent years. "It is not perfect," he adds, "but if you will take the time to put in accurate and thorough data, you can get an excellent idea of overall costs within an hour."

While not all of these tools are identical, net price calculators frequently ask for data like the following:

- previous year's tax return data

- adjusted gross income

- family context (i.e., siblings in college, custodial and noncustodial parental information)

- business owners—accurate income and assets

- divorced/separated/never-married parents: some schools will want information from both parents, regardless of marital status; in some cases, one parent is not and has not been a part of the student's life, so schools will need some details to waive that requirement

- complex situations (health issues/medical expenses, disasters, deaths, etc.).

Money Talks

In a fall 2018 NACAC blog post, Ashley Dobson provided helpful and important data for families:

- Only 0.2 percent of students get $25,000 or more in scholarships per year.

- During the 2015–2016 school year, $6.1 billion in scholarships was awarded to 1.58 million students. If you limit the data to students enrolled in bachelor's degree programs, it works out to be one in eight students who received an average of $4,202.

- Just 1.5 percent of students in bachelor's degree programs received enough scholarships and grants to cover 100 percent of the cost of attendance. Another 2.7 percent got enough to cover 90 percent of the cost of attendance, and 5.9 percent got enough to cover 75 percent of the cost of attendance.

- Only 2.3 percent of students in bachelor's degree programs receive athletic scholarships, averaging $11,914 each.

"When parents initiate conversations about finances early, students deeply value that respect and are way more aware, responsible, and interested in making college choices that make financial sense," says Ron Diaz, director of student awards, Stanford University. Conversely, anxiety and frustration are born out of a lack of knowledge, and the money wedge is driven deep when parents are unwilling to have a "cards-on-the-table" discussion about finances.

The money wedge is driven deep when parents do not have an earnest discussion about finances with the student.

Any admission or financial aid director can share countless painful stories about families in April of senior year who come to their office in tears. Having received their financial aid package, the reality of paying for college is upon them, and in most of these cases, they have not had earnest conversations along the way. Now, after the student has been offered admission, bought the college hoodie, and changed all social media profile pictures to indicate intent to attend, financial lines are being drawn and emotions are running high on all sides.

The money wedge is real but avoidable. We encourage you to sit down as a family at some point in the student's junior year and have an initial discussion about your finances. While you do not need to itemize all of your finances, we encourage you to provide perspective on your financial situation and how it relates to paying for college by covering some of these topics:

- monthly or annual earnings

- taxes

- fixed/consistent costs (mortgage, insurance, car payment, utilities, groceries, tuition if attending a private high school, organizational membership fees, donations)

- savings (retirement, future purchases, health-related expenses, and college costs)

- lifestyle (a second home, vacations, entertainment, eating out, trips to visit family and friends).

Parents, we understand that this may feel uncomfortable initially. However, walking through how you afford the life they have known has tremendously positive implications. While most students have discussed politics and perhaps studied micro- or macroeconomics, a personal discussion around taxes and monthly expenses helps frame their understanding in a completely new way. Most students have no idea how much an average monthly mortgage payment costs and have given no real thought to how their college tuition compares to your home value and financial obligations.

"Opening the books" shifts the financing-college conversation to a partnership and a collective investment. As their first significant adult decision, students should be privy to the expense and implications of their college choice. These talks will help you have better discussions about opportunities to offset costs through jobs, co-ops, or internships. They will help you ask good questions of the colleges in which you are interested, about return on investment, careers, salaries, and how they help their students pursue employment opportunities within specific majors during and after college.

Our hope is that after walking through family finances hand in hand, you will be on the same page about how paying for college education fits into this broader framework. You should have a ballpark idea of how much your family can pay annually excluding any student loans. However, there is a fundamental difference between the ability to pay and the willingness to pay. This is where the conversations can get very emotional if you do not intentionally discuss limitations, conditions, expectations, and loan tolerance.

Limitations

What are you willing to pay for? Particularly in states with strong public university systems, we often hear parents say, "I am willing to pay for any of our state schools or the equivalent price, if my daughter chooses to go to an out-of-state public or a private school." Going back to our example of Duke and UNC, this would mean that after aid is awarded, the net cost of Duke would need to be around $24,000. Parents should consider and honestly discuss what limitations they want to establish. We are not suggesting that this keep you from visiting or applying to a school that looks like it will cost more than your determined threshold, but setting these limitations during junior year will keep you from feeling "gut punched" in April of your senior year when financial aid packages show up.

Conditions

"My parents will not pay for a school south of Washington, DC." Or "They have already told me I'm on my own if I look at schools in Canada." Or "We will pay for $40,000 a year for College X, but we are simply not paying that for Y University." Or the most alarming: "We will only pay for a college that is ranked in the top 50." (Don't be that parent.) What are your conditions? College is an investment. Your family's goal is to be comfortable with, and ideally excited about, the dollars you spend, because you believe in the experiences and opportunities you will receive. If you can talk about why you are putting conditions in place, they will not come across as irrational or arbitrary but rather as helpful, instructive, and ultimately rooted in concern and love.

Expectations

What role will/should students have in paying for their own college education? Even if your family is fortunate enough to be able to pay all costs, is there an expectation that students will contribute a certain amount each year? We have worked with families who have determined a flat amount, some who have set a percentage, and others who have defined a ceiling and left any additional cost for students to cover. Is there an expectation of shared costs for your family? In most cases, paying for college requires sacrifices—and sacrifices (physical, time, or monetary) bring some discomfort. However, they also clarify your commitment and belief in the end result. Setting clear expectations before you apply allows students to consider how they can work and save money during high school, as well as ask colleges they are interested in attending about opportunities for on-campus jobs or the prospects for—and salaries associated with—internships or co-ops while in college. Setting expectations will serve to further unify your family because "the problem" of paying for college becomes a joint effort—one to solve and resolve together. We recommend that even if families can afford to pay for everything, the student be expected to invest something—even if just spending money or covering books— so that they have a vested interest in their own success.

Loans

Currently, the average student loan debt nationally is approximately $30,000 (The Institute for College Access and Success 2017). With an average starting salary of approximately $50,000 for four-year graduates (Korn Ferry 2018), you should be asking questions around your comfort level for incurring loans on an annual basis during college, as well as what repaying loans at $300–$400 per month will look like after graduation. Parents, this is an incredible opportunity to discuss your philosophy on, experience with, or personal observations of the risks and benefits associated with taking loans. We have both worked with families who are completely averse to taking on debt yet are unable to simply write a check for all college costs. Those families can have very clear conversations about college options and financial aid requirements. What is your annual or cumulative student loan tolerance?

Direct PLUS Loans (also known as Parent PLUS Loans) allow parents to borrow directly from the US Department of Education and take out the cost of attendance (determined by the school) minus any other financial aid received (Federal Student Aid 2018). This means that in some cases parents are borrowing more than $30,000 to finance their student's education. Is that something your family is willing to do? Again, knowing this is an option, it is important to have an early conversation around *limitations*, *conditions*, and *expectations*.

Comparing Overall Costs

Look at the list of schools you wrote down at the end of chapter 2. Take some time to plug your information into those schools' net price calculators.

- How do they compare? Make yourself a spreadsheet so you can look at them side by side.

- Does your perspective about any of the schools you are considering change based on your understanding of expected costs?

- Have an initial discussion around your limitations, conditions, and expectations—and revisit these before you apply to colleges and again once you are offered admission so that everyone remains clear and on the same page.

- Discuss your student loan tolerance. Assume your starting salary upon graduation is close to the national average of $50,000. Build a budget, similar to that of your parents. What does life look like if you take out various loan amounts?

We also encourage you to check out the financial aid guide provided by the NACAC to learn more about more resources to facilitate the process of applying for aid. Some families find it useful to consult a financial advisor or use resources available in state-sponsored financial assistance programs.

WEDGE #4: EGO

We know this is much easier said than done, but for the sake of your family's relationships, we are urging you to put your ego in a box during your admission experience.

What Surrendering Ego Looks Like for Students

When letters inviting you to tour campus or attend an information session in your hometown arrive or brochures show up in your mailbox from schools you think are not "as good" as where you are hoping to attend, check your ego. Have the confidence to think for yourself. Be willing to consider places nobody in your family or school has gone before. Come back to your *why* and let that, rather than the noise around you, guide your opinions and approach. If you are able to articulate this confidently to your parents, they will both trust and respect your ownership of this.

When you are looking at the admission statistics or historical admit data from colleges and see that your academic profile is in the middle or lower end, we implore you to listen to your counselor and submit at least one or two applications to "likely" schools. Check out the cinematographic "masterpiece" *Dumb and Dumber* in which Lloyd Christmas (Jim Carey) asks Mary Swanson (Lauren Holly) the chances of them ending up together. He suggests "one in a hundred," to which she replies, "I'd say more like one in a million." Christmas pauses, considers, and then replies exuberantly, "So, you're telling me there's a chance!" Translation: applying to more schools with exceedingly low admit rates does not improve your chances of getting in. We have established that there are lots of great options out there. Do not let your pride or ego keep you from opening those doors.

When your parents want you to visit or apply to a certain school, keep an open mind. Listen. There is a lot of emotion tied up in this entire process for your folks. They are starting to imagine a life where they do not get to wake up every day and see you or hear your laugh or wait for your car to pull into the driveway at night. So, when they want you to check out their alma mater or swing by and visit a school they wished they had applied to, ask yourself why you are resistant. Is it because that college is completely contrary to your goals and interests? Fine. Look for a kind, tactful, thoughtful way to express that. Is it pride, ego, or simply being a contrarian? This wedge grows when you are not humble enough to acknowledge that and find compromise.

When Mom or Dad wants to "look over your essay one more time," remember it is because they love you. This is their way of showing that. Yes, we know that sometimes feels like a lack of trust or a desire to control things. Again, you have to remember that old habits die hard. They sang you to sleep for years that you do not even remember. They paid for over a decade of [insert instrument or sport of choice here] and loved you enough to make you stick with it, even when you pushed back. They have always hoped your life would turn out

> For the sake of family relationships, parents and students must put their egos in a box during the admission experience.

better than theirs and sacrificed amounts of time and money you will never know (and yet not viewed that as sacrifice). You are the last thought on their mind before they go to sleep (and frequently the reason they wake up in the middle of the night). Copious loads of laundry, endless debates about bedtimes, and countless teacher conferences—they love you more than you could ever, ever possibly imagine. Just let them look over (not rewrite) the essay.

What Surrendering Ego Looks Like for Parents

"Well, you know. We live in [La Jolla, Georgetown, Cambridge, Kirkland, Bethesda, Manhattan—insert your neighborhood here] and we went to [Yale, UVA, Williams, Northwestern, Berkeley—insert your alma mater here]. So I know you are saying there are lots of good schools out there, but most of those are just not OK for our family." We hear some version of this all the time—after presentations, in emails, over the phone, during individual meetings—this idea that because you live somewhere specifically or have a family background at a certain college (or type of college) there is a natural hierarchy and many/most "other" places are just not good enough.

When you say this kind of thing, whether it be off-handedly over dinner or directly to a tour guide or admission counselor, your son or daughter internalizes that. They feel increased pressure to succeed academically and distinguish themselves outside the classroom. The truth is that, on some level, all kids naturally have that inclination (whether they express or convey it is a different story), so hearing your comments only compounds anxiety about meeting your expectations. We are not criticizing your desire to see them perform well, but the problem—the wedge—is that they associate your approval and your love with an outcome: admittance to specific, and typically very popular and selective, colleges.

This is divisive because students cannot control admission decisions, the competition within a given applicant pool, or the specific priorities and factors those colleges are using. You deepen the wedge because they soon realize that what you expect of them, despite their best efforts, is ultimately not in their hands. Additionally, the school(s) you are focusing on may be completely counter to what your child is really looking for in a college. Each year admission offices receive essays or short-answer responses from students that say, "Please do not admit me. I did not want to apply and do not want to come there, but my parents have made me." (Yes, this really happens.) We have seen some pretty creative ways to work this into applications, including limericks, code, and parenthetical statements.

One that stands out was a student who applied to Georgia Tech a few years ago. Our speculation was that he could not work his lack of interest into his essay for fear that someone would proofread it and catch his intentional sabotage, so instead he used the biographical section (and capitalization) to reinforce his point: "Mother: Bachelor's Degree from College of Charleston (where I really want to go). Father: Bachelor's Degree from Georgia Tech (WHERE I DO NOT WANT TO GO!)." This same issue often continues into college. Advisors on campus frequently talk to students who want to change their major but are reluctant to do so because of parental pressure.

When recruitment materials arrive or you are having conversations about which schools to visit, or when your son or daughter adds certain colleges to their application list, we again urge you to "look beyond what you see." Fundamentally, this is about trusting your student to make good choices and being willing to engage in honest conversations about your fears, as well as your hopes and dreams for them, but also listening to and considering theirs as well. We are urging you to really listen to what your student is saying about why they want to go to college and be objective in considering the places that logically fit based on those goals.

> Really listen to what your student is saying about why they want to go to college.

When you hear them express interest in "the University of X" and associate it with the place that people went when you were a student if they could not get into [name more selective college here]. When you recall phrases like "If you drove slowly down Main Street with your window open, they'd throw a diploma in." When you remember that as early as Tuesdays people were already tailgating for Saturday's game. We are asking you to reassess "the University of X" and not lean on potentially dated perceptions. The landscape of higher education has been changing radically in recent years. That college town may be commonly written up in major national magazines as a great place for food, family, culture; they may have invested heavily in student support and programs; they may now have students winning international competitions for research and prestigious scholarships and fellowships. Resist the dismissive, knee-jerk comments like "party school" or "diploma mill." Change your filter. Do not dilute their excitement with comments or facial expressions that indicate you disapprove. *Your goal is to fall in love with every college they choose to apply to—all of them.*

When admission decisions are released, remember that they are not a validation or condemnation of your parenting. This may seem ridiculous to read before your student applies to college or receives decisions, but every spring we receive calls from parents of denied students who are struggling with "what more they could have done" and second-guessing their decisions about the high school they chose, a divorce, or a relocation and job change. When your kid does not get into a college (spoiler alert—that is going to happen), do not make this about you. Do not look back over the last 18 years of lost sleep and believe for a moment that a college's decision has any significance or correlation to your love, sacrifice, or influence.

Conversely, when they are admitted or receive a scholarship offer or honors college placement (yes, even if it is from your alma mater's biggest rival), celebrate. Go to dinner as a family. Reflect on the hard work, late nights, and collaborative effort that have brought this about at each school to which they are accepted. "Yeah, but it's only [insert school name here]." No! No! Another new world of opportunity has been opened and offered. That letter is an invitation to a network and a degree that many talented students will never access. Your student needs to know that for each of the schools they have an opportunity to attend, you will proudly wear that T-shirt and show up excited for Parents Weekend every year. Selectively celebrating only specific acceptances will show your hand and indicate your bias to your child at a time when they are attempting to discern their own independent feelings.

When financial aid and scholarship packages arrive, remember that every school has a different overall cost, endowment, and enrollment strategy. Do not allow your ego or desire to brag about a scholarship at a cocktail party to cloud your math. Each year we see families select one school over another because of the difference in the amount of aid awarded rather than the difference in actual cost. Here is the summary of how this sounds:

Parent: "Awesome University" gave us—oops—my son a
$20,000-a-year merit scholarship. "Congratulations College"
named him a Dean's Disciple valued at $65,000 over four years.
And you . . . you gave us nothing!"

University Representative: Well, sir, first, congratulations. I know you
are extremely proud of him. However, we do not have an Honors
College or merit scholarships here. You will see that we have
attempted to create a package that makes it as affordable as
possible for your son to attend—and we hope he will.

Nobody gets off that call feeling great. It may be honest, but it is
disheartening. Robert Barkley, the former director of admission at
Clemson University, used to say, "If you don't get in, you want in. If
you get in, you want money. If you get money, you want more. And
those who got in and got all of the money want it from somewhere
else."

Part of the reason why the admission experience can be so stressful is that it puts two things you always worry about together: money
and your kids. Understandably, it is not easy to keep your emotions or
ego in check when analyzing costs of this magnitude. If relative costs
are similar, you have the financial means to pay, and you have the confidence in your financial investment in a particular college, we urge
you to ensure your family is making choices based on best overall
match rather than the size of a scholarship or the ability to put a particular window decal on your car.

Parents, we suggest that once a week during senior year you make
time to tell your student: "I trust you and I am proud of you." The truth
is that all "kids"—whether 5, 15, or 50—long for their parents' approval.
They may find increasingly effective ways to hide or mask that desire,
but invariably it is there. Do not forget that the only reason you are
reading this book is that your kid has worked hard to this point. They
have achieved both inside and outside the classroom. You are worried
about admission decisions and financial aid packages because those
things are imminent. What a great problem to have! You are the only
one who can say it, and they need it more than they will ever let on, so
be sure you tell them frequently, "I trust you" and "I'm proud of you."
Simple, but tremendously important!

Try This

Consider the wedge you are most concerned about and take some time at one of your weekly college meetings to discuss why. Revisit these regularly. Is any of this going to ensure admittance to a first-choice school or give you an edge on a merit scholarship or honors college appointment? Absolutely not. The truth is that these wedges divide families when "getting in" supplants "staying together" as the primary goal.

 Talk About This

1. How do you foresee these wedges (time, communication, money, and ego) being a challenge for your family and why?

2. How will you go about addressing a wedge when you identify that it is becoming a problem?

3. Are there other wedges that you foresee hindering your family from having a healthy and unified college experience?

CHECK IN After reading this chapter, are you still on the same page? If you are not all-in together, what do you need to do, discuss, or learn to get there?

PART II

CHAPTER 4

Creating a College List

I really want to know (Who are you?) /
Tell me who are you?
"WHO ARE YOU" BY THE WHO

Keep an open mind that this is an opportunity to learn more
about your child's true interests and deeper desires. It's also
an opportunity for your child to declare those interests and
desires by making the college choice their own choice.
A PARENT'S ADVICE ON THE COLLEGE SEARCH

Imagine that your name is drawn in a local lottery. You have the option to choose a round-trip plane ticket or a helicopter tour. If you choose the plane trip, your natural focus will be all about where you are going. Destination is king. In the airport and on the plane, you will be surrounded by people singularly focused on their trip. They are headed to weddings or funerals, going to graduations, traveling to make speeches and presentations, visiting family or friends, or interviewing for a new job. Everyone has a precise end point in mind. As a result, delays are annoying, lack of coffee or spotty internet service is irritating, and turbulence is scary. What you remember about plane trips typically are the inconveniences—the amount of time it takes to get there, the uncomfortable seats, poor snack selection, and annoying passengers constantly bumping you as they head to the bathroom or remove something from the overhead compartment. What do you remember if the flight is smooth and arrives on time at its intended location? Nothing. Taxi, accelerate, take off, and land. That is all.

If you choose the helicopter tour, you will lift straight up off the ground with little effort or fanfare. Blades spin, seat belts buckle, doors close, and headphones go on. You are quickly airborne. Your focus is not where you are headed, because you know it will end in the exact spot it starts. The point of the ride is not to get somewhere. Instead, it is to see, learn, explore, appreciate, and to gain a new perspective.

The same is true of college admission. This is not intended to be a direct flight. Too many families view the college search and admission experience as a plane ride. They have one specific destination in mind, so they strap in tight and hope not to be annoyed, frustrated, or rerouted along the way. Our hope is that you begin to view it as a tour. Your goal is to look beyond what you see, to rise up rather than barrel down the runway, and to spend your time excited and learning rather than anxious and trying to control all the details or stay on an exact route.

This chapter will help you enjoy and appreciate the ride; give you good questions to ask along the way; help you look down over the landscape, observe your choices, and see things from a different perspective; and most importantly allow you and your family to "fly" together.

FIRST THINGS FIRST

The stress and anxiety people describe when they discuss college admission centers on the piece of the experience that you do not control—where and when you will be admitted and how much money that school will give you to attend. It is easy to forget that you control two-thirds of your college admission experience: where you visit and apply, and ultimately which school you select to attend.

In the next section of the book, we will cover how you can put your best foot forward in your application. First, it is important to add another important building block to your firmly established foundation stone—matching your *whys* with *wheres* in order to create a logical list of colleges to visit and apply to.

If you will continually remember the helicopter ride and keep an open mind as you explore different options, your list will be continually changing. Do not be disconcerted. That is precisely what you want.

FRESHMAN AND SOPHOMORE YEAR

We are often asked, "What should I (or what should my student) be doing in ninth and tenth grades for college?" The short answer is, "Not much."

At this point, your job is to be a good high school student. Take classes that interest, challenge, and prepare you. Be a good member of your school and community—not because you think it is going to help "get you in" but because being involved is what makes a rich, rewarding, memorable high school experience. Yes, colleges are going to look at your impact and influence outside the classroom, but you should be volunteering your time, working, participating in clubs, or playing on teams because you are in exposure mode at this point. (Note: we are not suggesting you have to do all of these things.) Do what you enjoy. Try new things. If you hate tennis, do not join the team just because you think it will help you "get into college." First, it will not. Second— there is no second.

Parents, please encourage your children (and frequently remind yourselves) to enjoy these all too brief and precious years. Resist the temptation to turn each event and grade into a discussion about their college "resume."

Keep it simple: Ask yourself some basic but invaluable questions: What do I choose to do when I have free time? What genuinely interests and excites me? What do I like to read or research on my own? What do I have the most fun doing? What am I good at? What would I learn and explore even if it were not required in school? What kind of people do I enjoy being around? What parts of my state or country interest me or would I want to live in? What jobs or professions appeal to me and why? Keep asking these questions and making notes as the answers change. Tara Nelan, formerly a college counselor and now the regional director of admission for Muhlenberg College, puts it perfectly: "Being authentic and honest with yourself in answering these questions, especially during the 12–20 months leading up to you actually submitting an application, can help your journey through high school to college be one of growth instead of a task to be done."

Look and listen: As a ninth and tenth grader, you are in a great position to be a casual observer. Don't miss out on this chance. Watch the juniors and seniors in your school, on your teams, in your clubs, at your job, or around your community. Listen to their conversations and deliberations. What are some of the colleges that the kids you admire are visiting and applying to?

What about some of the adults in your life? Relatives, coaches, friends' parents, leaders in your community, neighbors—what do they do for a living? What about their life interests you or seems appealing? Where did they go to college? As you get older, you will be hearing the incessant question, "Where do you want to go to college?" Get out in front of it. Ask them now where they went and why? What would they do differently knowing what they do now? They will be thrilled to give you advice and insight, if you will initiate the conversation.

Go: Early in high school, we recommend simply getting on college campuses either close to home or while traveling on a family trip. Make an effort to see the campus of a big public state university, a small liberal arts college, or a technical or art institute if you are interested in those fields. Walk around, watch the students, subtly eavesdrop on conversations, catch a game, wander through buildings, eat in the dining hall or food court or at a popular restaurant on the edge of campus. Get a feel for the size of different colleges and how they connect with the surrounding community. Again, ask simple questions: What stands out? What do I like here? What would I not enjoy if I went here? Your answers are hugely important because they point you toward the qualities you will be looking for in the future.

JUNIOR YEAR

This whole college thing is probably seeming a lot more real at this point. Breathe.

Separate needs and wants: In his book *Start with Why*, Simon Sinek introduces the "Celery Test." Sinek suggests that you imagine that you attend a dinner party and at the gathering a number of people approach you and tell you what they think you need: M&M's, Oreo cookies, and celery, to name a few. These recommendations come from highly accomplished, successful friends. When you go to the supermarket, you spend a lot of money buying all of these products, some of which will have little or no value to you. Sinek explains that if you know your *why* before you go into the store, you will make better decisions. If your *why* is to be as healthy as possible, you will leave the store only with celery (and saved a lot of money).

> Identify your *needs* in a college versus your *wants*.

Identifying your *needs* in a college versus your *wants* is critical. Is being able to double major a *need*, or would a minor in one of those areas be OK? Would it be *nice* to have easy access to go see professional sports or Broadway productions or eat in world-class restaurants, or are those experiences *imperative* for you? Maybe you hope there will be a rugby team or a marching band. Ask yourself if those are complementary elements or absolutely central and absolute deal breakers for you. Becoming confident in separating *needs* and *wants* will help you tremendously in this process.

BEGIN WITH THE BASICS

Location: Ultimately, your goal is to find a college where you are excited and confident about becoming part of that community. This starts with figuring out the type of setting (rural, suburban, small town, urban area), culture, or part of your state or the country that you are naturally drawn to. Weather is a big deal. Snow looks great on brochures and social media but walking around in sub-20-degree weather for months on end is a different experience. If you are from Miami, visit Vermont in February, not June. Conversely, if you have never experienced humidity, go to New Orleans in August.

Consider some helpful questions like these: Do you need or want to be able to drive home often and quickly, or are the costs and limitations of flying back OK? How important is the size, layout, and architecture on campus? What types of restaurants, activities, or cultural events do you want to have access to on a regular basis? Do you need specific health care access?

Size: Are you more comfortable with a smaller college of fewer than 2,000 students or would knowing everyone in your class by graduation seem confining? If your high school's graduating class is 50–100 students, your perception of what a large college is will likely be different from a friend whose high school has close to 3,000 students. On many campuses, you will need to take a bus or shuttle between classes. Are you comfortable with that, or do you want a more intimate and compact campus where everything is walkable?

Not all colleges of similar size feel the same when you are on campus. For instance, if you are in the most popular major, your class sizes will likely be higher than their published faculty-to-student ratio, and that has implications for access to professors, research opportunities, classroom dialogue, and more. Many large universities in recent years have invested heavily in honors colleges or living-learning communities that help create smaller, more intimate cohorts. Go beyond the overall enrollment numbers to determine what your experience would be based on your major and interests.

Majors/programs: One of the many reasons that college rankings are—at best—misleading is that the strength and breadth of specific program offerings at different schools vary greatly. The most selective college in the country might be amazing if you want to study biochemistry, but if they offer only one elective in your intended major of animal behavior, name and acceptance rate are irrelevant. If you are undecided on your major (like most applicants), you may want to explore colleges that allow or require you to explore broadly among disciplines. Given that well over half of undergraduate students change their major at least once (Straumsheim 2016), you should also find out what each college's policy is on switching majors. Practices vary widely. Some schools allow students to change programs without any limitations. Others require you to apply to specific majors after a year or two on campus. Some colleges have GPA requirements or other internal transfer processes for their current students to change from one major to another. This is critical information with significant implications that too few students think to dig into before arriving on campus.

People: Who do you want to be surrounded by for the next four-plus years? Remember that a big part of going to college is creating a network of friends and colleagues. You may be a student for only four years, but the connections you make there will last a lifetime. Where do alumni from colleges you are considering primarily live and work? Find alumni magazines and school newspapers online and check out the social media accounts of student groups to get a sense of overall campus ethos.

How important is campus diversity to you? Where students are from and the backgrounds they have will strongly influence conversations over pizza at 3:00 a.m., as well as dialogue and debate in the classroom. Who are your people, your tribe, the types of individuals that bring out your best? These answers are hugely important to finding your best college matches.

Do you want a school that is known for student activism, conservatism, or community engagement? Is it important to you that most students live on campus? How do college athletics factor into the equation? Is evident school spirit and bonding with classmates by attending games part of your vision for college? College brochures may all look the same, but campus cultures vary widely.

Outside the classroom: When people say "college," you are probably not thinking about lecture halls or late nights in the library. This makes sense because most students are only in class or lab between 15 and 20 hours each week. Double or even triple those numbers to account for studying, writing papers, and so forth, and you are still left with a lot of time to do things you want to on campus and in the area. What are you excited about beyond academics in college? What do you want your college experience to look like in the times and spaces between the classes? Do you want to study abroad in a certain country or region of the world? Are you planning to have an internship or co-op in a specific industry or with a particular company? Intramural sports, clubs, ROTC, research, and service offerings all vary from school to school. Are you a hiker, climber, biker, or caver? How active are the outdoor clubs at the schools you are considering? If you want to pursue an engineering degree and study in another country, make sure this is possible. If you want to play a specific sport, are walk-ons eligible to try out for the team? You can find all of this information online and through social media. You should also make an effort to ask current students these questions when you visit campus.

Cost: A college's published cost should not keep you from visiting or applying, but you must understand the amount of financial aid you will need to make that place affordable to attend. As we discussed in the previous chapter, finances can be a significant wedge. We sincerely hope that you will consider our advice and have open discussions about earnings, expenses, savings, and how college costs factor into your family's overall financial situation, lifestyle, and goals.

Selectivity: We intentionally left this piece until last, and we hope you will as well. If you honestly ask and answer the questions we have outlined, you will find many colleges (with widely varying selectivity) that match your criteria. This is great news because you want to have a few colleges on your list where your grades and test scores put you above their average accepted student profile. There is nothing wrong with including a few schools with single-digit admit rates. However, if those colleges constitute your entire list, you are setting yourself up for disappointment. Again, your job is to keep an open mind—a mix of idealism and realism.

Research: College Board, Princeton Review, College Data, College View, College Raptor, Unigo, and others all provide free online interactive tools that allow you to enter and modify key components (size, location, cost, academic and nonacademic programs) to discover and compare colleges. Your high school may also have a college search and application management platform like Scoir or Naviance. If you are staying open in your approach, we expect you will easily identify 20 schools that closely align with your criteria.

RANK THE RANKINGS

Given the rising cost of tuition and increasing debt for many college graduates, it is understandable that families increasingly think of themselves as consumers in this process. While traditionally schools have avoided language that describes tuition as a transaction or the cost of a degree as a purchase, in recent years questions surrounding return on investment (ROI) have become far more prevalent. In response, colleges are focusing their marketing, presentations, and communications on "outcomes" for their students as much as they are on the student experience. In other words, they are attempting to articulate the short-term value of attending and also the long-term dividends that a degree provides. This is a good thing. ROI should absolutely be one part of your equation in making a college choice.

The downside of viewing college in monetary terms is the temptation to begin to quantify, order, and draw lines. This is understandable, because in our culture we are surrounded by lists. We will add a Top 50 playlist to our online music account in a heartbeat. Reviews and metrics dominate. Think about it. You cannot

> Rankings can limit a healthy and comprehensive college search.

turn on the TV or radio without hearing ads touting how a new truck was rated number one for towing power or overall customer satisfaction. We pull up comparisons online about average miles to the gallon, safety ratings, and resale value. These can be informative. They can provide some context, but in the end, do you buy the car that ranks highest in fuel economy if you have a family of six and it is a two-door vehicle? Are you completely swayed by a top ranking in power steering or seat recline angle when the SUV will not fit into your garage? Do you accept those ratings and rankings as fact without researching how they were developed and categorized? We hope not.

Yet when it comes to considering colleges, students and parents do all of these things. They take rankings and ratings at face value. They reduce an entire college experience down to one number and assign it infinite comparative value by arbitrarily drawing draconian lines in the sand. Each year students tell us that they were counseled to only apply to schools ranked in *U.S. News and World Report*'s Top 25 or that they were pressured to only visit schools ranked in the Top 10 in a particular field; or their friends wondered why they did not apply to more schools on *Niche*'s Best Colleges in America list; or ultimately they were made to feel guilty and misguided if they did not choose the highest-ranked school to which they were admitted.

Because this mentality is so prevalent, we believe it limits a healthy and comprehensive college search. There are many rankings sources, but here is the methodology from *U.S. News and World Report* (Morse, Brooks, and Mason 2018) as an example:

35%—Outcomes (including social mobility, graduation, and retention rates): How good of a job is the school doing at retaining, supporting, and graduating students?

20%—Faculty resources: How do faculty salaries and the number of students in the classroom compare to other universities nationally?

20%—Expert opinion / peer assessment academic: What do academic professionals from other colleges (presidents, provosts, deans, etc.) and counselors on the high school level think about that school? (Often these individuals are not familiar with the schools they are rating, and/or the questionnaires are filled out by support staff.)

10%—Financial resources: What is the average per-student spending on instruction, research, student services, and so on?

10%—Student excellence: What is the school's admit rate, test score averages, and number of students coming from the top 10 percent of their high school?

5%—Alumni giving: At what rate are alumni giving back to their alma mater?

Understanding this is how rankings are determined, we encourage you to ask these questions:

- Do I care if a president (or their assistant) from one college looks favorably upon another (especially accounting for what we know about college competition)?

- Is a school's ability to pay a faculty member $2,000 more annually ($244/month or $8/day) of consequence to my college search and decision?

- Do I really think there is a difference in prestige/quality/experience between two colleges because of the three-spot difference that places one inside and the other outside the top 25? The top 50? The top 75?

- If a college is in an ideal location, has a dynamic student body, is a good academic fit, but ranks ten spots below another, should that number (based on the factors above) matter?

- If the school is outside the top 100 but is offering me a scholarship and has graduates thriving in the field I want to pursue, should I turn it down for a higher-ranked but less-affordable option?

When you apply to college, you trust that they are going to take much more than just your test score or GPA into consideration. You do not want them to rule you out by drawing a line that you happen to fall just below, despite your great grades, classes, and extracurricular impact. Similarly, we would encourage you to visit and apply to schools not because of a subjective number but rather based on how it matches your interests.

Opt in. Earlier in the book we discussed the way schools search for students. Search is a two-way street. If you are not receiving information from a college that matches your criteria, opt in. Go onto university websites and complete their electronic prospective student form. Typically, they are going to ask for basic contact information, as well as some of your academic and cocurricular interests. This is an excellent way to begin receiving more general information from campuses. It also puts you on their radar to invite you to campus for special visit programs and to inform you when they are coming to your city or school to conduct information sessions.

Visit. During your junior year, you should be taking the opportunity to hit the road. We will expand on the importance of, and best practices for, visiting colleges in the next chapter. Ideally you will visit every college that makes it onto your final application list, and often students need to visit twice as many colleges as they ultimately apply to. This might mean traveling to as many as 20 colleges, so start early. We understand that traveling to campuses is a big investment of both time and money. If you are unable to physically get to some of the places that interest you, check out the virtual tours that schools produce and present on their websites. YouVisit and CampusTours are among several companies that also partner with colleges to show pictures, videos, student testimonials, and online campus tour information that can be helpful resources.

Show up. Colleges' admission representatives travel extensively in the fall, and increasingly in the spring, to meet students and build excitement for their college. Keep an eye out for college fairs in your area. These can draw reps from several hundred schools who gather to speak with prospective students and families. Regardless of location (stuffy gym, crowded cafeteria, cavernous convention hall), you will find a space lined with admission officers standing behind folding tables and displays with their school banner, glossy brochures, and often some free swag. College fairs are a great way to gather information, network, and learn about schools you have not yet considered. Do not waste this opportunity. It will be crowded, and your time with each college will be limited. Be prepared with two or three questions to which you could not easily find answers on their website. Schools often have forms to complete or will point you to web links where you can share your information. Do this. It is an excellent way to receive follow-up information about majors, application tips, or campus visit programs and maybe even earn you points for demonstrated interest.

> College fairs are a great way to gather information, network, and learn about schools.

Similarly, when colleges come to your high school, make every effort to attend. Do not just passively receive information. Use that time to connect with the admission officer (typically the same person who will be reading your application). Again, do not let them simply go through their canned speech. Be sure to get your specific questions about your needs and wants answered. Having presented to hundreds of high school groups, we can attest that admission officers greatly appreciate students who ask these types of thoughtful, detailed questions.

Whether you are reading a college guide, looking online, or taking advice from a sibling or teammate, remember that this is *your* search, *your* list, and nobody else's. No one person's opinion is the absolute truth about a particular school—no alumnus, current student, admission director, or college president. Your job is to solicit as many opinions as possible and look for trends and commonalities while staying connected to *your* needs.

LATE SUMMER AND EARLY FALL SENIOR YEAR

Trust your gut. Are you excited about schools you had not heard of a year ago? Have some colleges dropped off your list even though you bought their T-shirts when you visited campus? You are on the right track. Has the order of your list changed? You are doing this right! Remember Sinek's "Celery Test" from the beginning of the chapter? Look at your "shopping list." Confirm again that all of the colleges you are still considering align with your interests, values, and priorities—your *why*. Did you really not like the campus, or did you just have a bad tour guide? Did you sour on a school that was interesting at first because of an offhand remark from a peer? Remember, it is *your* list, *your* choice, *your* college experience.

Apply. Our advice is to arrive at a final list of colleges that is between five and nine schools that ideally answer your *why*. We advise you to break down your final list as follows:

- 2–3 "reach" schools—colleges where your grades and scores put you below their average admitted-student profile

- 3–4 "target" schools—colleges where your profile aligns with their average admitted student

- 1–2 "likely" schools—colleges where you are well above the average admitted-student profile. (While you may hear the term "safety" school, there really is no such thing.)

In the end, the driving question is this: Would you be excited to attend every school on your list? Barbara Tragakis Conner, the director of college counseling at Foxcroft School in Virginia, advises that students apply to five first-choice colleges. The point is that each school on the list should be a great match where you feel as though you could be happy and successful—this way you will not be disappointed if you are not accepted at any given institution.

Unlike the traditional college fair, at Kentucky Country Day School's Finding Your Fit Fair, college admission officers leave the literature behind, as well as their name tags and banners. Each representative is then asked to submit a list of five distinct characteristics or programs at their university, which are printed on a bland white sheet of paper. Students wander from table to table focusing on the programs or experiences the colleges may offer. Next, students and admission officers gather as a group to debrief the experience, at which time they reveal the names of schools where each representative works. They discuss what the students—and admissions officers—learned, what surprised them, and how their preconceived notions were challenged. Finally, they allow the college representatives to return to their tables (with brochures, literature, banners, etc.) and meet with students again. This format encourages engagement and discernment rather than reflex and judgment. It is the ideal approach to building a college list—one that focuses on values, programs, and the experience. Consider ways you can conduct your search in a similar manner—focusing less on name and more on how the schools match your criteria.

> The ideal approach to building a college list is to focus on values, programs, and the experience.

NEEDS	WANTS

Share your current list among family members, and answer questions about why each school was included. Ideally, there will be some overlap but also different colleges on each list. What are the commonalities? Differences? What can you learn about each other's expectations, hopes, goals, and priorities based on these lists?

 Talk About This

1. What outside influences are going to affect the college list you build? Rankings? Family connections? Finances? Friends? Parents and students should both make a list and then share your responses.

2. What is one thing you need to communicate to your parent/child about the schools being considered?

3. What resources are you going to rely on for information about colleges? Are they objective or subjective and how?

CHECK IN After reading this chapter, are you still on the same page? If you are not all-in together, what do you need to do, discuss, or learn to get there?

CHAPTER 5

The College Visit

I hope you never fear those mountains in the distance /
Never settle for the path of least resistance /
Livin' might mean takin' chances, but they're worth takin'.
"I HOPE YOU DANCE" BY LEE ANN WOMACK

Parents be cool. Students relax. Both enjoy the moment.
You're on a college campus where possibilities and
opportunities are boundless. Trust your gut and you'll
know the moment when it's the best place
for you to thrive.
JEFF KALLAY, RENDER EXPERIENCES, FOUNDER AND PRINCIPAL

As we pushed the faded motel sofa in front of the paper-thin door, I (Brennan) knew this was one of those father-son moments that I would never forget. We were in a questionably safe motor lodge in upstate New York that looked as though it was right out of a 1970s police drama. While at the time I expected an escaped convict to kick in the door at any second, this is now just one of many great memories I have of my week-long college tour with my father. Similar memories abound from the trip that my mother and I took months before. On that adventure, my brother and I had spent the week desperately trying to convince her that she didn't need to ask the tour guides if girls were allowed in the "boys' dorms."

Despite the inevitability of a few missed flights or meals or highway exits, we hope these trips will be memorable. We hope they will be the source of stories 3, 5, or 15 years from now that start with, "Do you remember when" or "Can you believe that we." Our hope is that you will look at this as an adventure; a time to explore, connect, and enjoy these experiences together.

WHY VISIT

Visiting a wide variety of schools—large, small, urban, rural, private, public, near and far from home—is the best way to separate your needs and wants that we discussed in chapter 4.

Would you buy a car without test-driving it first? Would you rely solely on consumer reports or simply trust in the brand? When speaking with students and parents, a former colleague, Bruce Berk, compared a year of college to buying a car every fall and then driving it off a cliff in the spring. This analogy is fitting in so many ways. It is up to the student whether they are going to park their car passively or spend the year getting the most out of the driving experience. Just as you would not buy a car sight unseen without a test drive, it makes little sense to choose a college without running it through a checklist of features and experiencing it firsthand—you need to try before you buy.

While websites, videos, social media, and virtual tours can be helpful, there is simply no substitute for visiting campus and getting a sense of the school, its programs, and its community. It is also an important way to demonstrate to an admission office that you are sincerely interested. Increasingly, institutions are using "demonstrated interest" as one criterion in their review of candidates. Admission professionals want to know that applicants have done their research and are applying because they are informed and therefore more likely to enroll if an offer of admission is extended. Visiting campus is one of the best ways to do this.

> There is no substitute for visiting a campus to get a sense of the school, its programs, and its community.

WHEN TO VISIT

Students frequently ask, "When am I supposed to start going on college tours?" And the response is simple: "When you are ready." As we outlined in the previous chapter, you may want to begin exploring campuses early in high school, or you may have to be prodded by parents as senior year approaches. The most important thing is that you have the willingness and openness to experience a campus and to be intentional about the visit—this timeline is different for everyone. There are no rules that dictate when you should or should not visit a college, but there certainly are best practices that the informed "consumer" should keep in mind.

The ideal is to visit colleges when school is in session and students are on campus. A weekday tour and information session and/or interview will provide the best feel for the campus, culture, and community. Many colleges offer Saturday-morning tours, but it will likely feel deserted until midday when students reluctantly start to emerge like groundhogs in February. Since summers and high school holidays are among the busiest times for college visits, planning ahead will make it more likely that you can schedule tours and interviews while they are available.

If the college does offer on-campus interviews, take advantage of this opportunity when you visit as a junior or senior. Some families do an initial tour of schools to see where the student is interested, and then they return to interview. Do not postpone this opportunity: it is a waste of time and resources to have to return to each campus. Interviews are a great way to get to know a college, and if the school doesn't end up making the final application list, at least it is good practice for a valuable life skill. We will provide some helpful tips for the interview later in the book.

HOW TO VISIT

Most colleges have a "visit" link on their website that outlines the different opportunities to get to know their institution. Usually you can book visits online or with a simple phone call. If a school allows you to sit in on a class, we highly recommended you take advantage of this opportunity—the more ways to experience college life at each school, the better. Do not try to pack too many visits into one day or week. Be conscious of travel time, and give yourself space in the schedule to process and enjoy time as a family. Do not attempt more than two visits in a day, and more than five or six visits in a week will likely leave your head spinning. Try choosing a common theme to experience in each town. One student and his father made it their mission to find the best burger restaurant nearest to every college they visited.

CRITICAL QUESTIONS

Traveling to visit colleges is a big investment of time and money. You have already seen how similar college emails and brochures can be. Campus visits can be even worse because you are literally sitting through hours of PowerPoint presentations and watching tour guides walk backward as they talk about the exact same topics: volumes in the library, the ability to study abroad, how you and three friends can find a faculty member and start the juggling club. If you do not intercede and ask your questions, you can expect these to blur together until each admission officer and tour guide sounds like the voice of the schoolteacher in Charlie Brown cartoons: "Wah wah, wah wah, wah, wah." It will seem like everyone has a great biology program, and you will start to hear, "Sure. You can double major in English and sound design. That's extremely common." Mary Wagner, the assistant vice president for enrollment management and executive director of undergraduate admissions at the University of South Carolina, advises families to ask, "What is the campus culture like? What do students think is important, and do I agree with much of what they get worked up about? Which place makes me feel most welcome? Can I see myself fitting into many of the activities and academic pursuits that current students enjoy?"

Asking the right questions, and being persistent in asking, is a fundamental life lesson. As you go through the college admission experience, this is absolutely vital. Our hope is that when you visit college campuses, you will commit to being a relentless inquirer. Consider the following ways to reframe your questions for more depth of understanding.

Student-to-Faculty Ratio

You ask: "What is your student-to-faculty ratio?" This number may include faculty who are doing research, those who teach only one undergraduate class, and even those who are on sabbatical. Take a look at an online college guide like www.bigfuture.com or www.unigo.com. You will find that many schools are listed with ratios of under 19:1, students to faculty. Does that mean you and 18 friends will be sitting around a table in Introductory Calculus your first year? In most cases, the answer is no. These statistics include all courses and levels (including the courses with two students and those with two hundred), so while not entirely unhelpful, they certainly do not tell the whole story.

> When you visit college campuses, commit to being a relentless inquirer.

You *should* ask: "What is your typical introductory class size?" This question gets you right into the classroom. Schools rarely publish average SATs or GPAs but rather bands or ranges. Likewise, you want to look at their ranges and variances within class size. At Georgia Tech, as an example, the most common class size is 26–33, and around 7 percent of courses have over 100 students in them. The student-to-faculty ratio, in contrast, is 19:1. When you visit, ask questions around class-size percentages and ranges. That information will be far more helpful to you in framing expectations and determining what kind of experience you will likely have. Ask current students what their typical class size is, who teaches them (full professors, adjuncts, graduate students), and how accessible faculty are on an individual basis outside of class.

And *then* ask: "How does that vary from first year to senior year? Is the range higher or lower for the major(s) that I am considering?" You will find schools often have introductory-level classes like chemistry or economics with rosters four or five times higher than their averages. While not reflective of the entire undergraduate experience, it is helpful for you to understand the variance, because it is also the case that upper-level chemistry and economics classes are half or a quarter of the average.

Your job is to probe. Your job is to dig and to clarify.

Graduation Rate

You ask: "What's your graduation rate?" Colleges will have a wide variety of answers, and with national averages below 50 percent, you need to dig deeper. Some will give you their four-year graduation rate; some will provide a five- or six-year percentage. The variance is not an effort to be misleading or nefarious; they have been trained to respond with an answer that is most representative of their students' experience. Most private, liberal arts schools would likely not even think to provide a five- or six-year rate because there is no significant difference and their goal is to graduate students in four years. That is how they structure curriculum, and it is their culture. In contrast, some colleges have a high percentage of their students interning, working a co-op job, or studying abroad for multiple semesters. Many students take more than four years to graduate but only pay tuition for eight semesters.

You *should* ask: "What are your four-year and six-year graduation rates? At those two intervals, what percentage have either a job offer or admission to graduate school?" This will help you understand their outcomes. You will find that some colleges have a high graduation rate but low placement or graduate school entry percentage.

And *then* ask: "How does the graduation rate vary by major? What percentage of students who double major, study abroad, conduct research, and/or have an internship finish in four or six years?" Your goal should be to learn whether graduates are leaving with a broad network and opportunities rather than whether they finished four years after someone hit start on a stopwatch. Often the reason graduates take more than four years to graduate is because they have used their time to gain work experience, contacts, and global exposure that translate to lower loan debt and higher earning potential. At that point, who cares about the clock? You might even ask, "How many students finish in less than four years by taking advantage of summer offerings or other special programs that allow them to save money and/or time?"

Retention Rate

You ask: "What is your first-year retention rate?" This is a great and important question. The national average for students returning to their college for their second year is typically around 65 percent in four-year colleges. Therefore, when a school reports that their first-year retention rate is 85 percent, it sounds impressive.

You *should* ask: "Why are those other 15 percent leaving?" Is it financial? Is it because the football team lost too many games? Are the students who leave disproportionately in certain majors or from out of state? Is it because the school is too remote or too urban or too big? Your job is to dig deeper. Ask them to articulate who is leaving. Schools should know these reasons. Some schools have retention rates below the national average, but they are losing students who are successfully transferring to state public flagships or into specialized programs in the area. These answers provide context beyond the bottom line number.

And *then* ask: "What resources are there on campus for academic student support?" Many colleges have invested significant human and financial resources to ensure a positive campus experience. Is there an office dedicated to retention, intervention, and enrichment?

A VARIETY OF VOICES

When you are visiting schools, your goal is to acquire a combination of answers from a range of sources so that you can get a balanced perspective. No alumnus, tour guide, faculty member, or current student has a corner on the market of that school's entire story. College and universities are vast. Experiences vary widely. Even the president is not the expert on all things for that campus. Ask the *same* questions to as many people as you can.

What makes this college different from other schools? This question is essential. If a student, tour guide, admission counselor, or faculty member cannot answer that question, *run!* One of the most challenging parts about the college admission experience is discerning how one school stands out from the other 4,000 in the country. If you find some common themes despite varied experiences, you have likely found the school's real identity and can consider whether that resonates with you. In contrast, if you find an inability to articulate a unique culture, it should give you pause.

What is the most exciting thing happening on campus? Perhaps the answers are all about sports and you are not much of a fan; or they are focused on a major in which you are not interested; or they center around political activism, the new vegan dining options, and the 16-screen movie theater, but you are an apolitical carnivore who has a fear of loud noises and big crowds. All of this is helpful. This is what *match* is about: campus culture and ethos. In contrast, maybe the answers are all about the incredible start-up culture or the ways students work together to solve problems or the emphasis on students having an international experience, and those are your passions. Congratulations! You have broken through the noise and found a real match.

What question has not been asked today that should be asked? We suggest asking this at the end of a tour, information session, or interview. This gives the presenter an opportunity to hit on something that really matters to them. The good news is that this will not be scripted, so you can count on it as being authentic, honest, and reflective of their priorities.

What do you wish you had known coming here? Ask this to students, tour guides, and even to professors or admission staff who may not be alumni. Are these responses generally positive? Comments like how "surprised" they were by the number of hiking trails in the area or variety of good restaurants near campus. Or are they predominantly negative? Warnings about how expensive it is to live in that area or that there are not direct flights to most places. These responses will give you great information to consider as you make your decision to apply or attend.

How has this college set you up for success and fulfillment in the future? We suggest you ask this of first-year students, as well as seniors, while you are on campus, and also later of recent graduates and alumni who are well into their careers. This is also a pertinent question for faculty and upper-level administrators. Are you hearing answers like, "the incredible network" or "the phenomenal reach and reputation" or "the ability to think critically and work collaboratively toward solutions." Do those answers resonate with your goals?

Bonus questions: What has disappointed you? What do you wish were different? What is the most frustrating thing you have run into? Where do you see this school in five years or ten years?

Understanding context and gathering a more complete story is your goal for college visits. Do not spend all of that money and time to travel and be absent from school just to accept the answers that colleges give you in their presentations or tours. Do not be too shy to ask questions. Be resourceful and use your networks to find individuals to share their experiences. Maybe this means your friends' parents or your parents' friends, or perhaps your counselor can connect you with former students from your high school. Online resources can also be helpful in building connections. Social networks have made this extremely easy. As a student, this is *your* job. This is *your* college choice and experience. So it is not your mom's job, and it is not your counselor's job. *Your* job. *Do your job!*

> Understanding context and gathering a more complete story is your goal for college visits.

Here are a few other ways we suggest you use your time on campus to maximize your visit:

1. Develop a list of questions that you want answered at each school about academic programs, as well as life outside the classroom. Some areas about which to inquire might be internships, career counseling, first-year retention, social life, safety, travel abroad programs, or other areas of interest/concern. (But don't ask, "How is your biology department?" because you will just get, "It's great!")

2. Try to connect with the admission representative who is responsible for your high school or the area where you live. If that individual is not available, ask for their contact information/business card.

3. Allow ample time to wander the campus after you leave the admission office.

4. Ask the admission office if you can have lunch in the dining hall.

5. Try to find a random student (not a tour guide) and ask their thoughts on the college, accessibility of professors, school

spirit, support structures (tutoring, writing centers, career resources, etc.), and what it is like to live in the area.

6. Stop by the academic department of a discipline in which you have interest to talk with a professor and/or student. Better yet, contact the department beforehand to see if you might meet with someone. Ask about their research or other special programs. Even if you cannot connect with someone in the department, see if you can find some examples of student work or projects on display.

7. Contact coaches, music directors, and others beforehand to set up meetings while you are on campus. Better yet, attend an athletic event or concert/production. This will give a good snapshot of school spirit and support for student initiatives and shows.

8. Pick up the student newspaper, as it generally offers an uncensored take on the issues facing students and the college as a whole.

9. At the end of your visit, ask yourself what story each college was trying to tell through the tour and information session. Is this consistent with what you value and the experience you seek? Can you see yourself as part of this story, and does the college align with the story of your life? What is "special" or "different" about the school? There are so many similarities between schools—it's good to know what distinguishes each school. Make some notes for yourself about this differentiating information, as it will all melt together if you don't have a record of your impressions.

BEEN THERE, DONE THAT: *VETERAN ADVICE*

Wisdom comes from experience, and we suggest heeding the sage advice of students and parents who have been down the roads of college visits and lived to tell about it. Here is what they had to say.

Students to Students

"Pay attention to small things . . . posters on the wall, how harried or at ease the students appear. Imagine the campus in the dead of winter (cold, dreary, miserable days, and would you want to be there); look for what social activities go on, look at the range of clubs and class sizes. Take advantage of any 'stay the day' or 'stay overnight' experiences."

"Get off the propaganda path. Eat at the cafe, read the student newspaper, wander around campus without the group, go to a class, talk to students you meet, etc. Visit as many colleges as you can in small bursts."

"Stay close to the tour guide so you get all the info during the tour. Don't be nervous about asking questions. Ask them why they chose that school—it usually says a lot about that place."

"Stay away from your parents during the tour! Make your own opinions about the school and do not let their impressions rub off on you. Same goes if you happen to be touring with friends. You can debrief on the way home or on the way to lunch!"

"Keep an open mind that there is something to be gained from each visit, even ones you found least appealing, because you learn what you like and what you don't like along the way. Make notes immediately after the visit, what was liked and what wasn't. When deciding which college to 'accept,' you might not remember details."

"Don't judge only by the tour guide. Don't be scared to talk to students that aren't tour guides."

"Take a virtual tour of the campus before visiting, so it feels familiar from a physical point of view, and you can spend your actual time there focusing on how it feels—the atmosphere, the people, etc.—rather than on amenities."

"Find a student that you have a connection with: a graduate from your high school, someone who went to your summer camp, your cousin's friend from high school, your club sports teammate's older sibling. Go to eat in the student center with that person, ask them all your questions about the school. You will get much better answers than from your tour guide and you will have a better idea of the background and perspective of the person answering the questions."

"Enjoy the journey!"

Parents to Parents

"Let your child be in charge; stay in the background."

"Start early (if the child is ready) as time is a premium as the student approaches senior year. Be realistic. Don't waste all of your time visiting schools that are a reach for everyone. Make sure you visit a mix of selectivity so that your child has more likely options he/she can get excited about. Have fun! Chill out and enjoy the time with your child."

"Ask your kid what they think of the school before you give your input so that they can develop their own opinion about the place before you sway their answer."

"If your child says they don't like the school, don't push them to stay and keep looking. Listen to your student. They are the ones who will have to live there."

"Visit colleges early in the process and use it as an opportunity to further build relationships with your child. Embrace the process."

Other Helpful Tips

"Asking offbeat questions at information sessions and tours. It throws off the propaganda agenda and you start to see truths."

"Having a tour guide who told a lot of stories about their experiences at the school was the most helpful way that I learned what life was like on that campus. It helped a lot to ask them for favorite moments or stories about their favorite class or experience."

"Don't try to convince yourself you like a school because it is a 'good school.' If you don't like it, you don't like it. Don't let the name cloud your judgment."

"When I first began my search, I knew nothing about what I was looking for in a college. The least helpful for me was going into a college tour without knowing what terms like 'LLC' or 'RA' meant, how a college class schedule typically worked, what a meal plan was, or what college dorms typically looked like. Basically, not doing enough background research beforehand was really the least helpful."

"Research smaller, lesser known schools when visiting an area; you never know when you might find a hidden gem."

"More than two visits a day is too much and all the schools end up blending together."

"You will never know everything about a college in a day, so have a goal to learn about your interests and where they sit within the college."

"When visiting, don't just visit the school and leave town directly after. Is there a town life? Is there something beyond the campus gates? This will help you decide if the area is right for you. For example, going to the Dr Pepper Museum with my mom after visiting Baylor showed us how interesting the town was but it also gave us a memory together and took away a lot of the stress I get when I visit a college."

"Students and parents, have fun with each other while it lasts and try to make college visits educational about the institution but also a fun time together. This is a great tradition to have while touring!"

"Thank-you notes. Beyond this being a good practice and a lost art today, it can't hurt a student's file."

☀ *Try This*

Scavenge. Who doesn't like a good game or challenge? A little creativity will turn your college visits into more adventurous and memorable experiences. Is your brain going to explode if one more time you hear how many books are held in a college's library or you endure another explanation of the blue safety light system common on most campuses? Why not create a scavenger hunt that will keep you alert, while allowing you to dig deeper into a college community and providing an innovative way to contrast different schools.

The items or challenges on your scavenger hunt will be uniquely yours depending on specific interests, areas of study, or other priorities you may have, but here are a few examples/suggestions to get you started.

- Collect a student newspaper from each campus.

- Find the name and location of the favorite late-night student hangout.

- Get a picture next to the most important landmark or statue on campus. (Many schools have traditions related to these attractions.)

- Collect a pen, postcard, or other common memento from each college.

- Take a photo of or with the school's mascot or its likeness. (Some schools make this easy, like the University of Richmond, with a life-sized spider in their admission center.)

- Visit an academic department that houses programs you are interested in and talk to at least one professor. You might build a list of specific questions you want answered about access to courses, intriguing internships, or graduate school placement.

- Come up with your own addition to this list and share it with friends.

The options are endless in terms of what you put on your scavenger list, but the more challenging the better, as it will encourage you to gain greater familiarity with each institution.

:Ö: *Try This (Extra Credit)*

Get lost. This final tip comes from Joe Greenberg, a former professor and retired regional dean of admission for George Washington University. He advised that one of the most effective ways to get a read on the culture of a campus is to identify one of the busiest hubs of campus life (maybe a quad, dining facility, or student center). Position yourself in the center of activity with a copy of the campus map, and do your best impression of a lost tourist. Next, wait and see how long it takes for someone to stop and ask if you need help or directions. Does everyone just navigate around you with earbuds in or eyes fixed on their phone? Do you get strange looks of suspect? Are you tackled to the ground by campus security? The reactions of those around you and your observations of what community members are engaged in will provide a window into the vibe of a campus.

 Talk About This

1. What role will each family member play in arranging college visits and trip planning?

2. What environmental factors might affect your visit in unexpected ways? For example, a rainy day, a really hot day, a tired or overly enthusiastic tour guide? How will you ensure that you look at and hear the bigger story of each campus?

3. What types of follow-up discussions will you have after each visit? Students, do you want your parents' impressions, or would you prefer that they withhold comment? What will you use to make notes, document pictures, and record lessons you learn from your visits?

🖒 **CHECK IN** After reading this chapter, are you still on the same page? If you are not all-in together, what do you need to do, discuss, or learn to get there?

PART III

CHAPTER 6

Admission Factors I

What Are Colleges Looking for Academically?

Gonna cruise out of this city / Head down to the sea / Gonna shout
out at the ocean / Hey it's me / And I feel like a number.
"FEEL LIKE A NUMBER" BY BOB SEGER

You have built a list, visited colleges, and refined your criteria, all while
staying united and balanced. You have successfully identified your
why, *what*, and *where*—now it is time to turn your attention to *how*.
There are three primary means of submitting a college application
(institutional-specific applications, the Common Application, and the
Coalition for College application), and while at times you have your
choice of all three, some schools only offer one or two of these options.

There are a handful of colleges and universities that require students to use their *institution-specific application* because they want to
have more control over the development and implementation of the information they collect from candidates. Some larger state university
systems also offer one proprietary application that students can use
to apply to multiple campuses.

The *Common Application*, established by 15 private colleges in 1975,
has grown to an association of over 800 member colleges and universities, both public and private, in the United States and around the
world who have collaborated to provide one universal undergraduate
application for admission (Common Application 2019). Students can fill

out a single application online and send it (typically for a fee) to as many schools as they wish. Many of the member schools also have supplemental questions or essays that accompany the Common Application, and those that offer their own institutional application must agree to give equal consideration regardless of how a student chooses to apply.

The *Coalition for College* was established in 2015 and has over 140 public and private member institutions. It is an alternative to the Common Application, though many schools allow students to apply through either application (Coalition for College 2018). Coalition member schools are united by their mission to support less resourced or savvy students and families, and hope to create access to an affordable college experience through associated online tools like a "locker" where students can store supporting materials throughout high school.

What does this all mean for you? Truly, if a college or university offers more than one option, they will not have a preference for which application you use. They are simply interested in obtaining accurate and thorough information about you, assessing your ability to thrive at their school, and determining how you will contribute to classroom discourse and campus life. If all of your colleges use a particular application, we recommend you save your time and energy and go with that one. You will need to be sure that you pay close attention to all institutional requirements beyond the standard application—that is, additional essays or other materials that are specific to each college.

> Pay attention to all requirements beyond the standard application that are specific to each college.

If multiple applications do not sufficiently confound you, perhaps an array of deadlines will. Undoubtedly, by the time this book goes to print there will be even more admission plans through which a student can apply, but here is a primer on the most common options and deadlines.

Rolling Admission: Under this plan, students may apply at any time after the application is open (usually late summer after junior year or early fall of senior year). Many colleges that offer rolling admission will try to review applications and render a decision on a specific timeline (i.e., three weeks after submission). These colleges extend admission offers on a rolling basis until all spots are filled, at which time most schools will still accept applications for the waiting list.

Early Decision (ED): This is a binding agreement through which a student can only apply to one school where they will commit to enrolling if admitted. A growing number of colleges and universities are now offering two rounds of early decision, the first usually in early November and the second in early January (allowing students denied at their first choice or who decide later to use this option). Most early decision 1 applicants are notified of a decision in mid-December, and early decision 2 applicants will learn of their decision in late February or March with the rest of the pool. There are even a few colleges that allow applicants to apply early decision on a rolling basis, meaning that at any time during the admission cycle an applicant can decide to enter into a binding agreement in consideration of their candidacy. Because admitted students are guaranteed to enroll, generally speaking, the acceptance rate for early decision applicants is significantly higher. Increasingly many selective colleges and universities are enrolling nearly half their class under this plan.

Early Action (EA): Like early decision, under early action admission plans, students usually submit applications in October or November and learn of their decisions in December or January. The main difference is that students are not bound to attend if accepted like with ED, and they can submit multiple EA applications simultaneously. While it varies from school to school, there is often a benefit of applying EA, because frequently colleges are taking larger percentages of their incoming class through this plan.

Restrictive Early Action (REA)/Single Choice Early Action (SCEA): OK, are you still with us? Remember how we just said that you can apply to multiple colleges through an EA plan? Well, there are a few schools that have developed a hybrid plan where students can apply and receive decisions early under a nonbinding application, but in doing so they agree not to apply to another school under a binding ED plan at the same time.

Regular Decision (RD): This is your standard, run-of-the-mill admission application with deadlines usually in early January or February and notification in late March.

Priority Applications: This can mean different things at different schools. At some colleges and universities, priority applications refer to an earlier deadline (often November 30 or December 1) by which a student can apply to be considered in the school's first round of review. This is often found at larger state systems like the University of

California. Priority applications are also sometimes called VIP applications, "snap apps," "fast apps," and a range of other names and refer to streamlined applications that encourage students to apply early (and boost a college's application numbers). Often application fees are waived and essays are not required.

Regardless of how or when you apply, this chapter helps you understand how colleges are reviewing your application.

HOW COLLEGES REVIEW APPLICATIONS / WHAT ARE COLLEGES LOOKING FOR?

Depending on the size of a college, the number of applications they receive, and their institutional priorities, the admission office will take one of two approaches to reviewing your application.

Formulaic Admission Review

Formulaic review is typically found at public universities that have determined that academic factors alone are sufficient to evaluate and enroll students who will be successful at their institution. Formulaic admission is based on just that—formulas that use the courses you take and the grades you earn (GPA) in high school, along with your SAT/ACT scores to assign you an admission "score." These processes are simple to understand because they are completely transparent. Think of the admission process at these schools like running the hurdles in a track meet. A university's primary goal is to ensure that the students they admit will be successful in the classroom. To do this, they evaluate the performance of their current students (college GPA, retention rates, graduation rates) and use that information to establish their school's admission standards. You are able to go directly to a school's website or admission publications to find the exact high school courses, GPA expectations, and standardized test scores that you will need to be admitted.

> With formulaic review, a university's primary goal is to ensure that students will be successful in the classroom.

A good example of formulaic admission is found in Iowa, where students can apply to the University of Iowa, Iowa State University, and the University of Northern Iowa with one application. Each school sets its academic requirements using what is known as the Regent Admission Index (RAI) (Board of Regents, State of Iowa 2019).

🖩 HOW TO CALCULATE YOUR RAI

Primary RAI Formula (for students whose high school provides class rank)

$(1 \times$ Percentile class rank)

+

$(2 \times$ ACT composite score or SAT equivalent)

+

$(20 \times$ Cumulative GPA)

+

$(5 \times$ Number of years of high school courses completed in core subject areas)

= RAI Score

Prior to applying, students can go to the admission website and use the online calculator to determine—based on their GPA and test scores—whether they will be admitted to each individual university. In Georgia, most of the state's public universities utilize the Freshman Index (the equivalent of Iowa's RAI). Here again applicants know the "height of the hurdle" in advance. They see it clearly and understand exactly what it will take to jump. This is not a timed event. Anyone who can clear the bar will advance (be admitted).

Arizona State University, Cal State, Penn State, and many other large public institutions, including a number of state flagships, operate with these models and enroll tens of thousands of students each year. The example in the figure below shows the Eligibility Index for the California State University system (Cal State University–Fullerton 2019).

SAT Eligibility Index Table of California High School Graduates or Residents of California

(A GPA of 3.00 and above qualifies for any score in SAT)

GPA	SAT SCORE	GPA	SAT SCORE	GPA	SAT SCORE
2.99	510	2.66	780	2.33	1040
2.98	520	2.65	780	2.32	1050
2.97	530	2.64	790	2.31	1060
2.96	540	2.63	800	2.30	1060
2.95	540	2.62	810	2.29	1070
2.94	550	2.61	820	2.28	1080
2.93	560	2.60	820	2.27	1090
2.92	570	2.59	830	2.26	1100
2.91	580	2.58	840	2.25	1100
2.90	580	2.57	850	2.24	1110
2.89	590	2.56	860	2.23	1120
2.88	600	2.55	860	2.22	1130
2.87	610	2.54	870	2.21	1140
2.86	620	2.53	880	2.20	1140
2.85	620	2.52	890	2.19	1150
2.84	630	2.51	900	2.18	1160
2.83	640	2.50	900	2.17	1170
2.82	650	2.49	910	2.16	1180
2.81	660	2.48	920	2.15	1180
2.80	660	2.47	930	2.14	1190
2.79	670	2.46	940	2.13	1200
2.78	680	2.45	940	2.12	1210
2.77	690	2.44	950	2.11	1220
2.76	700	2.43	960	2.10	1220
2.75	700	2.42	970	2.09	1230
2.74	710	2.41	980	2.08	1240
2.73	720	2.40	980	2.07	1250
2.72	730	2.39	990	2.06	1260
2.71	740	2.38	1000	2.05	1260
2.70	740	2.37	1010	2.04	1270
2.69	750	2.36	1020	2.03	1280
2.68	760	2.35	1020	2.02	1290
2.67	770	2.34	1030	2.01	1300
				2.00	1300

GPA below 2.0 does not qualify for admission

*For admissions purposes, the CSU uses only the SAT scores for mathematics and critical reasoning.

CSU SAT Eligibility Index Table.

Inside the Admission Office

I (Rick) am extremely familiar with formulaic admission because in 2003, when I arrived at Georgia Tech, this was the way we made the vast majority of decisions. That year we received around 8,500 applications for first-year admission. Our admit rate was approximately 62 percent—accepting basically two of every three applicants (Georgia Tech, Institute Research and Planning 2003). I loved traveling to high schools and college fairs during that time because the conversations were transparent and clear: "What is your GPA? What is your SAT? Yep. You will be admitted." We were operating on a formulaic, or "plug and chug," admission model. At that time, if you had a 1250 or higher SAT and a 3.7 or higher GPA, you were going to be admitted. We had room to accommodate students applying with those academic credentials. We knew based on our student data that they would do well. We ran the Microsoft Excel formulas, plugged admission decision codes into our student information system, and—voila! Change the toner, print the letters, grab a coffee, lick some stamps, and call it a class. Effectively, that formulaic process worked for us based on the admit rate, quality and size of applicant pool, and overall goals of the institute. It was easy, clear, and stress-free. The beauty of this was that it allowed a more direct and productive conversation, not about whether to apply based on chances of being admitted but whether a student *should* apply based on the type of college experience they were seeking.

A decade later, in 2013, after the recession, with return on investment (ROI) very much at the forefront of the nation's consciousness, families were asking much more pointed questions about outcomes (salaries, employability, etc.). Simultaneously, the science, technology, engineering, and math (STEM) tide was pushing more students into fields and majors that Tech offered. In that year, we received more than 17,600 applications (over 100 percent growth from 2003). Because we were not significantly increasing our first-year class size or undergraduate population, our admit rate dropped by one-third, to 41 percent (Georgia Tech, Institute Research and Planning 2013). Over the course of that decade, due to the sharp increase in both application quantity and applicant quality, numbers alone were no longer sufficient to make admission decisions. As a result, we moved away from formulaic admission to a holistic admission review process.

Takeaway: I am still in touch with many of the students who entered Tech when our admit rate was well over 60 percent, when we were not considered "highly selective" and applications were under 10,000. They have gone on to run companies, earn PhDs, and travel the world after selling their patented products—smart, successful, incredible people who are influencers in their communities all over the world because their work, pursuits, relationships, and network have led them to incredible opportunities. Remember these examples when you are evaluating colleges. Unfortunately, far too many applicants mistakenly correlate a college's quality with the number of applications it receives or their selectivity (admit rate). Students begin to believe (or are repeatedly told) that their future success and potential can be put on a corresponding spreadsheet and is directly linked to these numbers. Do not make that mistake as you are searching for and applying to college. Willard Dix, a Chicago-based independent college counselor and admission veteran, touched on this concept in his 2016 *Forbes* piece "Rethinking the Meaning of Colleges' Low Acceptance Rates," in which he states, "Although colleges love to crow about these numbers, they conceal a fact that few outsiders realize: A low acceptance rate, along with high scores, grades and other characteristics, indicates inputs, not outputs. It says nothing about what, how or whether students learn once they're there." Want more data? Check out the following table (on facing page) from the *Chronicle of Higher Education* ranking schools based on selectivity and student retention (*Chronicle of Higher Education* 2019). This is just a small sample of how admit rates do not correlate to retention rates or reflect the network, quality of education, and career outcomes of graduates.

Holistic Admission Review

If formulaic admission is like running the hurdles, holistic admission is more like judging a decathlon. John Barnhill, the assistant vice president for enrollment management at Florida State University, often jokes in presentations that holistic admission means that colleges "can do whatever they want and not have to tell you why." His quote illustrates that in holistic review, schools do not simply set a hurdle or a bar and accept everyone who clears it, because they receive too many applications from students who could do exceedingly well academically on campus. Others describe holistic admission as a blend of

Chronicle of Higher Education schools ranking

Rank	Institution	Retention rate, fall 2016	Number of students in fall 2015 entering cohort	Percentage receiving Pell Grants	Acceptance rate
1	U. of Wisconsin at Madison	95.40%	6,243	12.50%	56.90%
2	U. of Georgia	95.20%	5,240	20.00%	55.70%
3	Ohio State U.	94.20%	7,070	16.90%	53.00%
4	U. of Washington	94.00%	6,180	21.30%	55.20%
5	U. of Illinois at Urbana-Champaign	93.50%	6,926	21.30%	59.00%
6	Virginia Tech	93.40%	5,474	15.50%	72.60%
7	Pennsylvania State U. at University Park	93.20%	8,166	13.10%	50.30%
8	North Carolina State U.	93.20%	4,493	20.70%	51.60%
9	Rutgers U. at New Brunswick	92.60%	6,409	28.30%	60.50%
10	Florida State U.	92.60%	5,944	24.30%	55.40%
11	Clemson U.	92.30%	3,470	15.50%	51.50%
12	U. of Pittsburgh main campus	92.20%	3,845	14.90%	53.10%
13	U. of Connecticut	92.10%	3,577	19.00%	50.00%
14	Miami U. (Ohio)	91.80%	3,641	11.20%	65.80%
15	U. of Delaware	91.50%	4,522	14.80%	67.80%
16	Purdue U. at West Lafayette	91.50%	6,536	17.50%	59.30%
17	Michigan State U.	91.50%	7,890	21.40%	66.10%
18	U. of Massachusetts at Amherst	91.30%	4,691	20.90%	61.40%
19	James Madison U.	91.20%	4,358	14.90%	65.70%
20	U. of California at Riverside	91.10%	4,273	51.90%	58.30%
21	Auburn U.	91.00%	4,552	14.20%	83.50%
22	Indiana U. at Bloomington	91.00%	7,697	18.40%	76.10%
23	Texas A&M U. at College Station	90.60%	9,489	24.00%	71.00%
24	U. of Oklahoma at Norman	90.40%	3,882	20.60%	81.30%
25	U. of California at Santa Cruz	90.20%	4,019	40.50%	55.70%

science (objective quantitative evidence) and art (subjective considerations such as character, special talents, etc.). As a result, they have developed additional criteria for review and comparison in order to build and shape the class they want to enroll at their institution.

At universities utilizing formulaic processes, admission staff are primarily recruiters. They travel to college fairs, visit high schools, and deliver campus presentations, but because their decisions are numeric, human intervention, discretion, and influence is minimal. The opposite is true in a holistic process. While staff also recruit, much of their year is consumed with reading applications and making admission decisions.

> Holistic admission is a blend of science and art.

Behind the Holistic Curtain of the Admission Office

After you submit your application, the admission team ensures that your file is complete by matching your transcript, letters of recommendation, test scores, and other supporting documents. Some offices will read files randomly. In other words, once an application is ready, it is pushed into an admission officer's queue to be read that day. Other schools will read geographically, reviewing all the applicants from a certain high school, county, city, or state at one time. Traditionally, the first person to read your application is the individual who travels to your area and is charged with recruiting in that region. Their job is to understand your school and community environment both inside and outside the classroom. After they read your application, they make a recommendation to admit, defer, deny, or wait-list. They then pass it along to a second reader who also reads your file in its entirety. Often the second reader is more seasoned and, if they agree with the initial recommendation, has the authority to make a final decision. However, in some cases, your application will be passed along for a broader committee to review, discuss, and decide.

Each school reading holistically determines its own model for review based on application volume, staff size, and institutional priorities. At some universities, faculty are involved in reading applications, while at others they are thankful to never read a college essay. Some colleges move a file immediately from the "first read" into committee. Others use what is called "committee-based" or "team-based" review, in which pairs of readers sit together and review each application simultaneously, so they can discuss your application in real time and make their admission recommendation.

As you visit colleges and speak with admission representatives, you will usually find that they are clear about the particular process they use for making their admission decisions (if not, be sure to ask). Now we are going to help you understand what they are looking for, what questions they are asking each other as they review your application, and what types of conversations they are having in those committee sessions.

ACADEMIC COURSE CHOICE / RIGOR OF CURRICULUM

The first question admission readers ask when they open your application is, "Where does this student go to school?" They want to understand what curriculum choices you have. Does your school offer an AP curriculum, IB curriculum, neither, or both? What are the varying levels of rigorous curriculum in your school? Gifted, magnet, honors, advanced—the reader wants to understand the classifications that schools use to categorize their curriculum. To determine what you had access to in your school or community, they refer to the "school profile" that your high school counselor provides to accompany your transcript. If you have not seen this document, you can often find it on your school's website. For admission counselors, this is a gold mine of information and insight.

Regardless of what your school labels its courses, the admission counselor's fundamental goal is to understand *what you could have taken and what you chose to take* during high school. When you visit colleges or hear admission counselors speak, you will continually hear them say that they want to see "that you have chosen to challenge yourself." Often, however, they do not explain why.

Admissions readers want to see you chose rigorous courses in high school because it demonstrates your desire to push and stretch yourself. They see your choices, in a sense, as a character trait. Your preparation is also critical because college courses are challenging and professors want to know that you have had experience with the pace and depth at which they cover and discuss material.

In order to rate or evaluate the extent to which you have challenged yourself, some schools will literally count and record the number of "rigorous" courses (AP, IB, dual-enrollment college courses, etc.) as defined by your school's profile. Others have developed an internal rubric that categorizes classes and allows readers to rate the strength of your curriculum choices. Often these are simple, logical, and applicable to any high school. As you can see in the example below, this is not intended to rate the quality of a high school in a comparative fashion but rather evaluate individual choices within the context of a school's curriculum.

Example

5—Extremely challenging course selection in all classes

4—Strongly challenging course selection in all courses

3—Moderately challenging course selection in some or all courses

2—Less challenging course selection in some or all classes

1—Not academically challenging

Other fundamental questions admission readers will ask as they review your school profile:

- What percentage of graduates from the high school continue on to college (both four-year and two-year institutions)? This is one of the many ways colleges begin to determine the strength of the school.

- Are there limits on the number of courses students can take each year? For instance, in some schools, students are not permitted to take more than two or three AP classes each year.

- What is the highest level of each academic subject offered, and what courses are required for graduation? Understanding those two questions provides the reader insight about what is reasonable to expect in that school context and if required courses may limit choice or progression.

- Are classes "open access," or do students need to receive a recommendation to take them? In some schools, you cannot simply register for any course. Instead, a previous teacher may need to recommend you and strict caps can be applied to the number of students eligible for a specific class.

- Have students from this high school attended our college in the past, and how have they done? Many colleges will track student performance by individual high school as part of their review and use this in their evaluation.

- Did the student switch schools during high school, or did the grading scale or curriculum offerings change? When students switch schools, admission readers ask why that change occurred and what impact (if any) it had in terms of course choice and performance.

Note: Admission readers appreciate that most high school students do not get to pick which high school they attend. If you go to a public school, that decision is largely dictated by where you live. If you are attending a private school, the choice of which one was best for you likely included factors such as proximity, cost, opportunities, and culture. Before ever reading an essay or seeing a test score, admission readers focus on understanding *your* school context, *your* school's curriculum, and the choices *you* made within that framework.

Course Performance / Grades / Trends

The proliferation of different grading scales in our nation's high schools over the last decade has been simultaneously maddening and humorous to colleges. While there was a time when the 4.0 GPA grading scale, numeric 0–100 grading scale, or alphabetic A–F grading scale were the norm, the GPA iterations today are astounding. In the same applicant pool, colleges review students who have numeric scales to 80 or 100 or 120. They still see the traditional 4.0 scales, many of which are weighted (additional points given to rigorous courses), but ceilings of 5.0, 6.0, 13, and 15 points are now becoming more prevalent.

Not to be outdone by the numbers, the alphabetic grading scale has its modifications. Some schools still use the conventional A–F grading system, while others assign + and − to grades in order to delineate. In some cases, schools no longer issue the grade of D, so the scale jumps from C straight to F. In the years ahead, we fully anticipate that a G–K scale will pop up, because clearly A–F is proving to be psychologically damaging. Alas, some institutions, particularly independent schools, have fully embraced the entire alphabet rather than being hamstrung by the stratification of letters and now write narratives, instead of assigning grades, in order to describe a student's achievement. Emojis and GIFs are likely the next frontier of GPAs!

As you can imagine, for colleges using holistic admission it becomes challenging to publish helpful GPA ranges and averages or speak with precision about grades. (Imagine the student in the back of the information session or tour who has an 11.3 GPA on a 15-point scale when the admission counselors say that their average GPA is *only* a 3.7.)

Mike Sexton, the vice president for enrollment management at Santa Clara University, explains, "We ask, 'What have the students done with what's available to them at their particular school?' We get applications from over 3,000 schools around the world and have seen every conceivable combination of curriculum, grading and weighting. It's not the GPA that matters. It's what's behind the GPA that is important."

Regardless of your school's grading scale, here is what colleges are looking for to determine course performance:

- Grade distribution and number of students in the class: this provides admission readers with a percentage of the class receiving various grades, as well as a general sense of the range in which a school's top performers will land.

- Number of students taking (or scoring above a certain threshold on) AP exams or SAT Subject Tests: understanding standardized testing performance within certain subject areas provides admission readers with a concept of results beyond grades. Does the school issue extremely high grades and yet students do not perform well on these tests, or perhaps the opposite? Comparing academic performance trends to test results can be a helpful barometer.

- Highest GPA in the class: sometimes found on the school profile, this is a standard question that both students and counselors will complete on college applications. Again, this provides perspective to admission reviewers about a possible ceiling and is used for comparison in conjunction with both grading scales and grade distributions.

Note: In order to bring some level of standardization and comparison to their applicant pool, some colleges will recalculate your GPA based on their internal scale. This is a good question to ask when you visit.

Regardless of grading scales, recalculations, and weighted or unweighted GPAs, when it comes to assessing academic performance, college admission reviewers are asking and discussing a very simple question: "Has this student taken challenging classes and done well?"

> College admission reviewers ask a simple question: **"Has this student taken challenging classes and done well?"**

The other fundamental consideration is, "How did this student progress through high school?" This concept is known as a grade trend—did a student increasingly earn higher grades in more difficult courses as they moved through high school, or did they start out strong and then struggle academically? Admission reviewers are also taking note of anomalies—lower grades in a particular class, a dip in one academic semester, or other notable situations. The variety of reasons for those blips and recoveries vary widely, and you will have an opportunity to explain them in a section called "Special Circumstances" or "Additional Information," which we will discuss later in this chapter.

Takeaway: Colleges practicing holistic review will not simply be putting your GPA into a spreadsheet and sorting from highest to lowest to make admission decisions. Admission readers are making notes, comments, and highlighting your course choices and progression. Their assessment of your academic career in high school is nuanced, not black-and-white.

What Does This Mean for You?

Each spring, when the line forms outside my (Brennan's) high school counseling office and there is a backlog in my email inbox, I know it is course-selection season—quite possibly my least favorite week of the year. Students and parents of all grade levels seek out their college counselors with the hope that we will bless their course program and assure them that it will lead to the college acceptance of their dreams. While we share the "truth as we know it" from decades working in the admission profession, undoubtedly they leave our office frustrated that either we will not make their decisions for them or we are unable to give the answer they are mining for. Here are some of the questions we repeatedly hear that you might be wondering yourself:

> "Is it better for me to take the regular class and get an A or choose the advanced class and 'risk' a B?"

> "I want to drop my language class, but I also want to be admitted to a highly selective school. Will they care?"

> "Should my son take three or four AP courses to be competitive for admission?"

> "Can I double up in English and history and drop math and science senior year?"

> "My daughter is a recruited athlete, so she doesn't need to take advanced classes, right?"

> "The college's admission website says only two years of high school history / social studies required, so can I stop after US History junior year?"

As with so much in college admission, the answer is, "it depends." If you will be applying to engineering programs, a course program lacking in rigorous calculus or physics is a red flag in admission review. If you are considering a technical institute and you decide to double up in math or science at the expense of a fourth year of language, it will not raise as much concern as if you were applying to a traditional liberal arts program. There are, however, some universal truths that are worth considering now that we know what colleges are looking for.

You have just learned that context is everything for admission committees. They do not expect you to take every AP, honors, or advanced class that is offered at your high school. What they are looking for is intentional challenge in your course selection, so straight As without rigor suggests a lack of willingness to stretch yourself, a characteristic you now know colleges want to see.

Expert Advice

We want to see students continue to take challenging courses— math, science, English, social science, and a language. Some students also manage to schedule that sixth or seventh sub- ject—an extra language, science, or math. Avoid the tendency to coast through senior year by avoiding the subjects you are less enthused by. —Beverly Morse, former Associate Dean of Admis- sions, Kenyon College

It's not just the level or rigor of classes you take that matters, but also the selections you make in given subject areas. Though there can be some exceptions, we are usually looking for four years of all the core subject areas. Things like taking Calculus after Precalculus or taking Spanish 4 after Spanish 3 (what we call the progression of a curriculum) really do matter.—Owen Bligh, Associate Dean of Admission, Providence College

Selective colleges put a lot of weight (a *lot*) on applicants' cur- ricular choices, so not taking a class each year from what I call "the big 5" can be a deal breaker: English, math, science, foreign language, and social sciences. —Jonathan Webster, Associate Dean of Admission, Washington and Lee University

It's good to bend, but not break. In other words, it is wise to stretch yourself but not so much that one overdoes it and becomes overwhelmed. A father whose daughter was not ad- mitted recently asked me about her challenging high school experience. "What was it all for?" asked this father who saw his daughter's high school experience through the narrow lens of the college admission process, rather than through the broader lens of preparation for college and life. She is someone who is incredibly bright, accomplished and promising. She will do great things in college and beyond. She is very well prepared for what lies ahead. Her father had lost sight of the value of her high school experience, outside of a desired college admission out- come. The point of course rigor is to prepare for a smooth transi- tion to college and to prepare for more advanced coursework in college—not to use one's course selections as a means of being admitted to the most selective college possible. I think stretching is good preparation for a productive college experience. —Paul Sunde, Director of Admission, Dartmouth College

The theme is clear—selective colleges expect your high school preparation to be broad, sustained, and appropriately rigorous.

Practical Tips for Completing Your Application

You will be asked on your application to list senior-year courses, and be sure to do this accurately, especially if your high school does not include senior classes on the initial fall transcript. In the academic section, you will also have an opportunity to share any honors you have earned. If your school has an honor roll or a similar distinction, you can share that here. It is also a place to list National Honor Society, Phi Beta Kappa, or other academic affiliations or awards from high school. (Please don't list every honor since elementary school, even though you are understandably still proud of your fourth-grade writing prize.)

STANDARDIZED TESTING—THE NOISE IN THE NUMBERS

Op-eds, books, and documentaries have sought to criticize, support, unravel, or unpack standardized testing. Strategies, research (research about the research), advice, analysis, and criticism are pervasive, and large, highly marketed test-prep companies continually insert themselves into any conversation about these exams. Unfortunately, because there is so much information, there is also a lot of misinformation. The cost of taking these tests, combined with their length and the ungodly hour at which they are administered, only complicates the equation. Even beginning this section you may feel a little queasy as you envision number 2 pencils, a room full of bleary-eyed students, and a test proctor who is either equally displeased about being there or, worse, seems to take great pleasure in watching you endure this rite of passage. We get it.

Test Optional: The first thing you need to know about standardized tests is that not all colleges require them. In 2018, the University of Chicago, Colby College, and the University of New England (among others) went test-score optional, joining an ever-growing list of schools (over 1,000) that have determined that they do not need test results to enroll a class that will succeed academically on their campus. FairTest: The National Center for Fair and Open Testing keeps a regularly updated "Optional List" on their website: www.fairtest.org.

After the University of Chicago made their announcement, Jim Nondorf, the vice president for enrollment and student advancement, reported that three-fourths of their applicants were scoring above a 1480 SAT (32 ACT). With so many students bunched into an extremely tight range, tests no longer served as a reasonable way for them to differentiate between candidates. Among highly selective universities, those numbers are not unique. Due to this noise in the numbers that many selective universities also experience, it is highly likely that the test-optional trend will only accelerate in the years ahead.

ACT vs. SAT: Originally, the ACT and SAT were far more distinct in format and style, and their regional footholds around the country (SAT predominantly on the coasts and ACT in the middle of the country) further separated the two tests. In 2012 (due in large part to extensive lobbying for state contracts), more Americans took the ACT than the SAT for the first time in our nation's history. The gap widened in 2013, and in 2014, the College Board revised their test to look remarkably similar to the ACT. We often hear students speculate that colleges prefer one test over the other or want to see scores from both exams. Colleges, by and large, are test-score agnostic and put no additional emphasis or priority on one over the other. Admission committees are not debating or speculating about why you took a certain test.

For schools that do require standardized testing, like all factors in a holistic review process, they will be viewed, well . . . holistically. That means colleges do not rank which factor in their process carries the most weight, even though it is understandable that families frequently ask for that order. Think about it this way—testing probably matters *a little more* than most directors or deans typically admit but far less than most students or parents imagine. Colleges do not simply take your GPA at face value without considering course choice, school context, trends, and so forth. The same is true of testing—they will ask the following questions to help them understand your scores.

What are this student's highest combined test scores? Known as "superscoring," colleges combine your highest total of subsections from the SAT or ACT, regardless of administration date.

Example

	Reading Score	Math Score	English Score	Science Score	Composite
June ACT	30	28	29	30	29
September ACT	28	30	30	29	29
Superscored ACT	30	30	30	30	30

In this example, while the composite scores are the same, the subsections vary and superscoring allows a committee to take your highest performance into consideration. They superscore because, like most parts of college admission, they are looking to give you the benefit of the doubt rather than penalize you for a lower score. They understand that sometimes the school bus breaks down coming home from a band trip on Friday night before the SAT. After waking up on the couch 20 minutes before the exam with barely enough energy to pull on a shirt and eat a few crackers, you may score lower on the math section than you did previously. Superscoring is their way of saying, "We get that."

Is this student competitive within our applicant pool? When an admission counselor opens your transcript, they have an expectation—that you will have done well and challenged yourself. The same is true when they review your test scores. They are looking to see that you are in the same range as other applicants. If their college's middle-50-percent test-score band for admitted students is 1370–1460, they will *not* take note if you are within that range. Testing would simply be categorized as neutral (essentially a nonfactor). If your scores are well above their range, while not a guarantee of admission, it is certainly to your advantage. Conversely, if you are in the bottom 25 percent, their expectations for the rest of your application immediately increase.

While in formulaic admission processes, and certainly at colleges awarding merit-based scholarships purely off test scores, they are using *cut scores* (prescribed thresholds such as > 28 ACT), that is not the practice in selective, holistic reviews. Committees will read every application. However, the truth is that if your GPA and test scores are both below their normal class profile, do not count on your counselor being able to write you what we refer to as the "Lazarus recommendation."

How many times did this student test? While the vast majority of colleges are only going to be interested in your highest combined totals, there are an extremely small number of schools (including several in the Ivy League) that will require you to send your entire testing history. They are asking questions concerning your timeline, trends, and access. Did you take the exam four times in your junior and senior years, or was September or October of your senior year the only time you took the test? Just like questions pertaining to "how you got your GPA," they ask the same for testing. Testing, in these colleges, is taken as a body of work.

Is this student's testing in line with other applicants from their high school? Just like committees consider the curricular choices you made at your high school and how your GPA compares within that context, they also are going to be looking at your test scores relative to other applicants from your high school or region. Many colleges also maintain and incorporate historical data to compare current applicants to past applicants from your high school who are now on their campus.

They may be asking about your AP test results, SAT Subject Tests, TOEFLs, and other similar metrics. Some schools require these specific tests or give you the flexibility to send a combination of SATs, ACTs, or specific subject-area exams. Committees requiring specific subject tests have determined that those results have predictive value on their campus, so you can be sure they will be looking closely and evaluating your performance relative to their applicant pool, current students, and applicants similar to you in geography, major, and so forth. For schools that "recommend" or acknowledge that they will review these content-based tests, if you choose to send them, they are looking to see that your testing is in line with your grades and course choices. If a student has all As in high school but is consistently scoring 1s and 2s on AP exams, it is an indicator to the college about preparation and ability in a standardized environment. While there is not a firm expectation that you send these tests (read: optional really means optional), it is an opportunity to demonstrate both your knowledge in a content area, as well as your interest in that college by sharing your scores.

Takeaway: While the majority of colleges superscore and are truly only interested in your highest combined subscores, you should explore each individual website of the schools in which you are interested so that you have a clear understanding of their process. You will find that they typically do an excellent job explaining (sometimes in painful detail) their practices. As always, this is a great question to ask when you talk to an admission representative at your high school or when you visit their campus.

Hamilton (the college, not the musical) does an excellent job articulating their policies and approach to testing.

Hamilton will accept official or self-reported scores as part of a student's application for admission. Hamilton applicants will have a variety of ways to meet our standardized test requirement. They include:

- The SAT (Essay optional for redesigned SAT); OR
- The ACT (Writing Section optional); OR
- Three individual exams of your choice, selected from SAT sections, SAT Subject Tests, ACT writing, AP scores or IB final exams. One must be a verbal or writing/essay test, one must be a quantitative test, and the third is your choice.

OUR PHILOSOPHY

- Hamilton requires standardized testing because it is one of several valid predictors of academic success on our campus. However, please remember it is one of many factors that we will consider in our holistic review of your application.
- It is Hamilton's policy to select the testing options that will serve you best. Some students do better on the ACT than the SAT, while others excel in SAT subject tests. For this reason, we do not recommend any one test over another. We strongly encourage you to submit all of your testing to Hamilton and the Admission Committee will choose the best scores for you.

- We do not exercise testing minimums and a quick glance at *Hamilton's distribution of scores* for admits will demonstrate that candidates have been successful with a wide range of scores. Generally speaking, however, admitted students who score in the lower range of Hamilton's test scores are *exceptional students who compensate in other compelling ways.*
- While Hamilton's practice is to "superscore" tests (meaning that the Admission Committee will combine the best Math SAT score from multiple sittings with the best Critical Reading from another, and the same for ACT subsections), we will *not* superscore the new and old SAT sections together. (Hamilton College 2018)

What Does This Mean for You?

Your head is probably spinning: ACT, SAT, Subject Tests, APs, subscores, composites, superscoring, middle-50-percent, ranges—just unpacking standardized testing and how it applies to you seems like its own exam. Here is the reality: for some colleges and universities (especially many of the most selective) standardized tests are a necessary evil in college admission. While there are an increasing number of schools that no longer require testing as part of their review process, if you have your heart set on a college that still does, standardized testing is going to affect your candidacy. If your scores are well below a school's testing profile/range, unless you have a significant "hook" (impact athlete or other institutional priority), your odds for admission are likely not good. Rather than feel confined or limited by these numbers, there are ways to take back control. For some, this could mean buying a book and taking countless practice tests. For others, it is as simple as an online course or maybe just a daily email with a test question of the day. The options for test preparation are as diverse and plentiful as there are testing styles, from peer or professional tutors to group classes to Khan Academy. Some students see significant gains of over 100 points per section and others remain stagnant. The point is that you may have to "play the game" if you are applying to an institution that values high scores.

> For some colleges and universities, standardized tests are a necessary evil in college admission.

When confronting standardized testing, it is also important for you to acknowledge when you have done all that you can and to know when it is time to accept your scores as they are. When your scores are not increasing between test dates despite the hours you are pouring into studying, at some point it becomes an unnecessary exercise in frustration. Determine the cost/benefit of the time and resources you are spending on readying yourself for this one exam and return to your *why*. You might need to revisit your college list to make sure your scores align with the colleges to which you are aspiring. Or perhaps you will need to focus on those test-optional colleges that we spoke of earlier in the chapter. Also be aware that some test-optional schools require or recommend an additional essay or other submission to accompany your application. A few colleges have moved to "test flexible" policies where students can combine subscores from different tests to present the best portfolio possible. For example, a student might send an SAT math score, an AP English score, and an ACT science reasoning score as their testing profile. Remember, your job is to put your best foot forward, and if you are not submitting test scores, the admission office will weigh the remaining parts of your application more significantly as a result, so look at the whole picture of everything you are presenting and what story it tells about your performance and potential.

Make sure you understand what each college on your list requires in terms of testing, and plan accordingly. Though fewer and fewer colleges require SAT Subject Tests for admission, there are a handful that require (or strongly recommend) that students submit scores from these tests for general admission or for specific majors. It is your responsibility as an applicant to know the requirements and policies of the colleges to which you are applying and to be proactive about scheduling the necessary testing to meet these needs.

Practical Tips for Completing Your Application

The Common Application asks if you wish to "self-report" your test scores. If you are applying test optional to any of the schools on your list, simply respond no to self-reporting scores and then send official test scores from the College Board or ACT directly to the colleges that require them. If all of your colleges require standardized testing, it doesn't hurt to self-report your test scores on the application. In fact, increasingly colleges and universities are allowing students to share unofficial test scores with the understanding that if you are admitted and enroll, you will need to provide official scores. This saves applicants a lot of money and allows you to have more control over which scores the colleges receive.

 Try This

Create a spreadsheet with the colleges and universities that you are considering. List the test ranges, average GPA, and other academic criteria for each college. Based on these statistics and your current profile, identify whether each college is a "reach," "target," or "likely" school for you. Discuss as a family and with your school counselor to determine whether they agree with your classification.

 Talk About This

1. What about the way that admission committees are reviewing your grades and test scores surprises you?

2. How do you think your application will read in a holistic and in a formulaic review process? Which type of process do the schools you are interested in use?

3. Having read more about admission review, what encourages you? What concerns you?

👍 **CHECK IN** After reading this chapter, are you still on the same page? If you are not all-in together, what do you need to do, discuss, or learn to get there?

CHAPTER 7

Admission Factors II

What Are Colleges Looking for Outside the Classroom?

It's a little bit of everything / It's the matador and the bull /
It's the suggested daily dosage / It's the red moon when it's full. /
All these psychics and these doctors / They're alright and they're all
wrong / It's like trying to make out every word / When they should
simply hum along. / It's not some message written in the dark /
Or some truth that no one's seen. / It's a little bit of everything.
"A LITTLE BIT OF EVERYTHING" BY DAWES

In order to enroll students who will help their college fulfill its mission, colleges rely heavily on nonacademic or qualitative factors to make admission decisions. Although we hope chapter 6 helped you see that even grades and test scores are not absolutely black-and-white, this chapter focuses completely on the gray—and that can be disconcerting to families because it is difficult to understand. The good news is that through our research we have recently discovered the perfect formula for being admitted to all colleges, even if you are not competitive academically.

Write this down: two years of martial arts, volunteer work at your local hospital, two sports (one involving either a racquet or a court, ideally both), and—*no*, stop writing. There is no script or blueprint here, so we cannot provide you with that. We can help give you an idea of what colleges do value and how to use that information when you apply.

EXTRACURRICULAR INVOLVEMENT/IMPACT

Colleges spend a good deal of their time in committee trying to understand not only what you have been involved with but also the contributions you have made in your community during high school. They want to know what your week/year looks like in combination with your academic life and course work. The reason they care is because they are attempting to build a campus community that will advance the mission of their institution and enrich the experience of others on campus. In order to do that, these are the key questions reviewers are asking.

What Is This Student *Involved* with Outside the Classroom?

In our culture, regardless of your age, time is arguably our most precious commodity. As a high school student taking a full load of classes that come with homework, papers, and studying, this is particularly true. When colleges are reviewing your extracurricular activities, they look at them not only as reflective of your interests but also of your values. They are far more concerned with understanding how you are using your time when you are not in school rather than judging your choices. In other words, they are not splitting hairs between earning the rank of Eagle Scout or working 30 hours a week at your local grocery store.

What Is This Student *Investing* in During High School?

A pressure that students often feel is that they need to have "done it all" in order to appear "well rounded" to colleges. This is a big misconception. Do not forget—admission committees are made up of people. They have families, they go on vacations, and they have dogs. They know that we live in an increasingly specialized society. No matter what you do outside the classroom, the demands on your time are growing. Coaches, bosses, club advisors all want more hours from you in the week and more of your weeks throughout the year.

If you are a musician in the band, you likely have multiple-hour practices, competitions on weekends, camps in the summer, a mandatory class during school, and "optional" (not optional) practices for your specific musical section. The same is true if you play soccer or tennis or another sport: club teams, school teams, traveling teams, indoor, outdoor, tournaments, summer camps, winter camps, and the list goes on. Trust us—admission officers *do* get it. They *do not* expect that you have played three sports, worked two jobs, walked old ladies across the street every day before school, and on the side cured a few diseases. While they do admit well-rounded students, "pointy" students who are uniquely committed to one or two activities with a deep level of achievement and experience are also great candidates. Pursue what you love to do in and out of high school, and make that clear on your application. Conversely, if you hate playing tennis and you see no benefit in participating, stop. One more season is not going to be the make or break for your application.

> Pursue what you love to do in and out of high school, and make that clear on your application.

What *Impact* Has This Student Made?

Two students could list identical activities on their application and be read totally differently. One is simply showing up—"a joiner." He signs the list, shows up for meetings, makes a few signs, and gets his picture in the yearbook. He is on the Homecoming Committee, eats the bread in French Club, and plays on the tennis team. Two years here, one year there. He has been involved but has not made an impact.

Meanwhile, another student started working on the committee as a freshman and as a junior and senior was in charge of publicity. No official title, but he is able to describe the successes of his work. He helped the French Club connect with a class in Metz, France, online and began an exchange program between the two schools. He plays tennis year-round and also teaches younger players in the community. His impact is clear, and this is a big part of what committees discuss and analyze in their review.

Notice in these isolated examples that what stands out to admission committees is not the positions a student has held. Colleges have broadened their definition of "leadership" from simply focusing on ti-tles to asking about a student's contributions. You can demonstrate impact through added responsibilities at jobs, helping raise three younger siblings at home, or serving as the primary translator for parents. Impact is not photobombing the yearbook or sporadic and nominal involvement. Instead, it is exhibited by longevity and depth. Reviewers are essentially asking, "Will this student be missed when they are no longer part of that community?"

How Has This Student *Influenced* Others?

Ultimately, admission reviewers are considering how you use your time outside the classroom because they know that being committed in high school translates to being an influencer during your college career and beyond. They are looking for students who will complement one another in their skills, interests, and talents. Their goal and hope is that in residence halls and classrooms, on practice fields and in lab-oratories, and even over pizza at 2:00 a.m., that the students they se-lect will stretch, push, challenge, and enhance the experience of others on campus.

While scales and language differ from one university to the next, colleges will generally use rubrics to evaluate and rate your compar-ative longevity and commitment, as well as impact, investment, and influence. Here is an example:

Extraordinary (1): Major impact within school, community, or subject matter; influencer, intentional movement, with depth either as a leader or independently. Sustained activity and influence over four years in three or more major activities.

Strong (2): Strong involvement with some influence. Extreme depth in one or two areas or moderate depth in multiple areas. Sustained activity over three to four years.

Solid (3): Involved but lacking influence. Busy but hasn't demon-strated growth in involvement. Involvement that isn't necessarily sustained but rather pieced together over multiple years.

Average (4): Sustained activity over two to three years. Has some gaps in involvement.

Lacking (5): Minimal involvement. No sustained activity or evidence of influence.

What Does This Mean for You?

Involvement, impact, investment, and influence—no problem, right? Now you know what colleges are looking for, but you are staring at your computer screen, and the application asks you to distill your high school years down to ten activity slots. You are likely either thinking, "How can I possibly fit all my extracurricular involvement into this restrictive form?" or panicking because you can only fill four slots and you are sure that every other "competitive" applicant has ten activities to brag about. Instead of fearing that you will not measure up or that you will somehow miss out, consider what story you want to tell about what you have chosen to do and—you know this is coming—*why*.

The college application is your megaphone, so make sure your message is clear in your broadcast. Before you start filling in drop-down menus on the application, step back and make a list of what you do when you are not in class, how much you do it, and then write down for yourself the reasons for your involvement. Start with the activities that are most important to you (even if they are not the most consuming), and work down to the less critical involvement. It might look like this:

Model UN: 3 hours/week since 9th grade, because I love the interaction with students from all over and I am curious about global issues and debate.

Swim Team: 10 hours/week in 11th and 12th grades, because I enjoy being part of a team and my friends convinced me to join.

Grocery Cashier: 20 hours/week 10th–12th grades, because I have to contribute to college and also earn my spending money and finances are tight at home.

You get the point. Writing these out ahead of time will help you articulate the choices you have made. This will not only help you complete the application but will also be useful if you have the opportunity for an interview. If you have more activities listed than the application allows, look at the entries at the bottom of the list and determine if they say anything significant about your involvement, impact, investment, and influence. If not, omit them. If they do seem important to the story you are trying to tell, make the application work for you. Some schools allow you to upload a résumé. If you choose to do this, your goal is to keep that to one page.

Practical Tips for Completing Your Application

Don't add fluff. If you are struggling to find things to add, it means you probably should not add them. Listing "waste management officer" because you take out the trash for chores once a week is stretching it!

> Consider what story you want to tell about what you have chosen to do and *why*.

Don't assume. Many high school clubs have fun acronyms. That is great and creativity is encouraged, but the admission office doesn't have a glossary of terms. Use the second field in the application to give a brief summary if necessary. (You don't need to explain swim team: "I propelled my body through the water.")

Leadership. Yes, the application will ask for your position/title, but that doesn't mean it is a requirement or that your role was any less important. When possible, use numbers or other facts to highlight your involvement (e.g., "one of four members who . . .").

Time commitment. Give your best estimate of the number of hours/weeks you participated. They are not going to conduct an accounting audit to reveal that you are off by a week and three hours. Again, application reviewers want a sense for investment and how you spend your time.

Remember: quality over quantity. You do not have to fill all the boxes.

ESSAYS AND SHORT ANSWERS

Like standardized testing, entire books have been published providing tips about the college essay. Titles like "Writing a Winning Essay" and "Confident, Clear, Concise: College Essays That Worked" promise that by following their advice, your words will jump off the page and convince any admission reader that you must be part of their next class.

In presentations and individual meetings, we often ask students which part of the application makes them the most nervous. Understandably, they cite the essay and short-answer section—it is the last piece of the application that you still control; it can feel vulnerable and exposing; and you do not have an accurate sense of what colleges are looking for.

Close your eyes. Seriously, close your eyes for just a moment. We want you to think about your classmates. Think about those who have similar grades and classes to you—that is, similar rigor of curriculum and approximately the same GPA. We are guessing you have a decent number of peers in mind at this point. Now only keep in your mind those who likely have comparable test scores to yours. Great. Next, consider the ones who have similar involvement and impact to you outside the classroom. Again, not all the same clubs, sports, jobs, volunteer or paid employment, but people who, like you, have pursued and improved your community outside the classroom. While with each additional layer we added, the number of people you were imagining likely went down, inevitably you still have a few classmates in mind. If you can imagine several people you *know* who "look" similar in other areas, think about an applicant pool of 8,000 or 21,000 or 47,000. *That* is why schools include essays in their application. They want—and need—you to distinguish yourself. Your writing is important because it helps admission committees *hear* you in a unique and important way that is simply impossible in other areas of your application. You could say that the *test* of the essay is your ability to concisely articulate your point.

Here are some of the common questions readers consider when they rate your essay or comment on your writing:

- Did I gain new insight or understanding into the student's life, motivations, values, character, or intentions?

- Do I see evidence of growth, maturity, or self-awareness?

- Is this piece compelling, unique, reflective?

- Would this voice add value to our campus culture?

How are admission readers arriving at their answers?

They *are* reading quickly. At schools receiving thousands or tens of thousands of applications, 30–50 applications per day is a very common review expectation. This means that your first line and first paragraph need to grab the reader's attention. Many reviewers will read the first line of each paragraph or the first and last paragraph of your essay to get a sense of your style and subject. In some cases that is enough for them to rate the quality of your writing and determine whether the topic you have selected provides them new insight.

They *are* wanting to learn something new and deeper than what they have already been able to discover about you as a student, a family member, and a community member from reading your application. Your essay fills in the color and adds texture to that picture. They want to know what inspires and excites you. A wasted essay is one that only reiterates what they already know. Readers do not want an extended résumé. Your writing, unlike other sections of your application, supplies the *why* not the *what*. They help committees make notes about your character, your motivations, and your mind-set more than your accomplishments.

What Does This Mean for You?

The glow from the laptop reflects off his forehead as he stares at the screen with a pained look of paralysis. The application essay prompts are neatly copied onto the blank document. His mind races from topic to topic, each of which he dismisses immediately. The championship soccer game . . . too cliché. His meaningful relationship with his deceased grandfather . . . overdone. The first time he received a grade below an A on an English paper. . . . Reading the college essay topics for what seems to be the hundredth time, he searches in vain for an event, challenge, accomplishment, obstacle, interest, or talent. And so he sits with the cursor flashing. . . .

You can write and rewrite your college essay to death with multiple editors providing feedback as you try to get it just right. Ultimately, it is a test to see if you can get out of your head and open your heart. It is an exercise in exploring self—what makes you who you are, not who everyone thinks you should be. Who are you outside the constraints that are placed on you by school, parents, friends, and society? How do you demonstrate character in your own unique ways? Simple, right?

Here are a few tips for writing an authentic, effective college essay:

Ignore the prompts. If an application provides multiple essay questions (like the Common Application), don't read them first, read yourself. Most conformists will stifle their unique voice by attempting to respond to a specific prompt that the application provides. What results is often a generic statement that lacks energy or personality. Write the story that you want to express and then choose the prompt with which it best aligns. If a college does ask you to respond to only one specific question or prompt, by all means follow directions—and do not exceed the word count.

Don't repeat the question. Which of these sentences makes you eager to read more?

1. "There are a lot of events and realizations that have sparked personal growth for me."

2. "The smell of sweat filled the tiny room as I tried in vain to struggle free."

You want to grab the reader from the start. Do not write your way into the essay by simply restating the initial prompt or question. Instead, put the reader in the moment by painting a picture, and then elaborate on why it is important.

Jedi mind tricks. The college essay is not a test to see if you can read minds or anticipate what the admission office wants to hear. Plain and simple, they want to know about you, how well you write, and how self-aware you are. Write the essay for you, not them.

It's not us, it's you. Regardless of the topic about which you choose to write, be sure the essay reveals more about you than the other characters or places in the story. Erik DeAngelis, an associate director of admission at Brown University, advises, "Don't fall into the trap of telling us why you're a great fit for our school by telling us all about our school. We know our school. Tell us how you'd take advantage of the resources and experiences available. Don't spend precious word space impressing us with your knowledge of the school, rather present your argument for how you envision yourself participating in academic and social life."

Happily never after. The moral to the college essay is that there need not be a moral. You are writing a personal narrative, not a parable, so don't feel compelled to conclude with a lesson learned or a happy ending. You are sharing your story, not a fairy tale.

Always ask why. When you have finished a draft of your essay, read it over and ask yourself why you wrote it. If you cannot answer this question, you might not be going deep enough or painting a vivid picture of who you are and what is important to you.

Did your essay hit its mark? Have you effectively communicated who you are and what you value? The best way to tell is to have your parents or a friend give a draft of your essay to a colleague or individual who has never met you. Ask them to read the essay and then respond with three adjectives that describe you and a sentence that captures what they learned. Does it reflect the message you hoped to convey? If not, you are back to the drawing board. Imagine you were to print out your essays without your name on them and drop them in the hallway at school. Could a classmate pick that up, read it, know it was yours, and learn something new about how you think or see things? If not, then start over.

> You are writing a personal narrative, not a parable, so don't feel compelled to conclude with a lesson learned.

Managing editor. Colleges are not looking for grammatical perfection or a certain number of multisyllabic words. Yes, you should run spell check. Yes, you should have someone else edit and provide feedback to you on your writing. However, there is a fine line between a second editor and a second author. Parents, do not steal your student's voice by overediting or replacing "related" with "consanguine" or "a lot" with "plethora." Ultimately, compelling, memorable essays distinguish you—not in your word choice or avoidance of comma splices but rather by your unique, distinct voice. A colleague used to equate admission readers to bank tellers who handle money constantly. They know when it is fake, and they know when it is not yours. If you are funny, that's great. By the time they get to application number 36 of the day, of course they appreciate some humor. Not funny? Do not try to be funny in your essay, because there is truly nothing worse than the unfunny funny essay.

No shortcuts. Reviewers do not want to read what you could (or did) write for another school. Increasingly, colleges are asking in their short-answer questions or supplemental, school-specific portions of their applications, "Why us?" They want specifics. They want you to have done your homework. Why do you want to study at Colgate or Colorado or Colby or another college starting with C-o-l? Do not write the same for each. You should be spending time digging back through those brochures or websites or notes from their information session to give details on *why* that are related to specific professors, opportunities, or campus culture. Do your homework, because that is how your writing will be reviewed and discussed. Essays and short-answer responses are love letters. Be specific and detailed. Saying "you are pretty" is not going to cut it.

"Am I done?" This is what every student asks, seeking validation that the essay is good enough. You want to know if you should work on another draft or if your essay is sufficiently polished. You are never done, however, as we continue every day to write our story and find our voice.

In closing, Todd Rinehart, the vice chancellor for enrollment at the University of Denver, provides perspective, summarizing the intent of the college essay:

Students should know that while essays are important, they are rarely the reason a student gets admitted or denied. Students shouldn't feel the pressure of having to write a Pulitzer-winning essay to gain admission to their college of choice. With that said, they also need to know that an award-winning piece won't supersede poor academic performance. Most admission committees are looking for capable and competitive students academically—once academic ability is vetted, an essay plays an important role in helping committees build their class with interesting classmates and roommates. Committees aren't looking for the perfect essay, topic, or set of activities and achievements— we simply want an interesting, authentic, and well-written glimpse into a student's life.

ADDITIONAL/EXTRA/SPECIAL INFORMATION

On applications you will find an open-ended section that allows you to add information. This is often simply called "Extra Information" or "Additional Information" or "Special Circumstances," but some schools have more creative naming conventions. What are schools looking for in this section, and how do they incorporate that into the overall review of your application?

Significant life events. You had mono as a junior and missed the first two months of school. Your parents' divorce was finalized in the summer before senior year, but the end of eleventh grade was filled with turmoil. You moved three times during high school due to a parent's job transfer, promotion, or loss. Your school changed grading scales or did not offer a certain class in your junior year. These are just some of the examples we see in this section. Readers appreciate the perspective you can provide, and they will make notes or highlight pertinent pieces that they believe are relevant to their review and admission decisions, especially as it relates to overcoming challenges, persevering, demonstrating tenacity/grit.

Academic context. Readers want to know if your academic choices were affected during high school. Were there schedule conflicts because some courses were only offered at certain times? Was a class that you'd hoped to take canceled due to low enrollment? If you moved multiple times during high school, readers will see that on your transcript, but in this section you have an opportunity to tell them about the impact that had. Maybe your move prevented you from being able to take a certain course or begin on a particular curricular track. This is where you can elaborate.

Additional activities. If you are unable to demonstrate the extent to which you contributed because the activity section is too limited, you can expound here. You might detail a business you started, a fundraiser you launched and developed, or additional levels of achievement from an activity you listed. You should put your strongest, most compelling information first in the activity section, and do not feel compelled to use this section unless it is absolutely essential to convey the depth of your work or time.

In general, this section is your chance to explain pertinent *whys* or *what elses* that have affected you during high school. This is not the space for another essay. This is not intended to allow you a place to enumerate excuses or look for sympathy. Instead, readers evaluate this section looking for critical pieces of information that provide valuable context (inside or outside the classroom) that you cannot convey elsewhere on your application. If you believe you have something noteworthy to add, use this section. Most students do not need to utilize this section. Often applicants express concern over whether it will "hurt them" if they do not complete this section. Absolutely not.

What Does This Mean for You?

This is not your opportunity to wax poetic. The application usually allows for 650 words, but this is not a creative writing assignment. Use this space (if necessary) but be succinct. If the reader is wondering why you wrote it, you didn't need to. The old saying from the paper file days of college admission apply here: "the thicker the file, the thicker the student." If you find yourself justifying choices or making excuses, then reconsider.

You could use this space to put a URL link to some creative work you have done online or other information without which it would be hard for an application reviewer to truly know you. Two words: be discerning; don't tell us what we didn't ask for.

INTERVIEWS

Not all colleges will conduct interviews as part of their admission process. Those that do vary widely in format. Some colleges conduct in-person interviews on campus with an admission officer. Others will host interviews at a local coffee shop or at your high school. Alumni interviews, current student interviews, faculty interviews, online interviews, and scholarship interviews are also common. Regardless, if these are part of a college's process, they are taking valuable time to meet you, listen to you, and learn more about you. Here is what they will be looking for, noting, and discussing later in committees.

They expect you to be prepared. Interviewers want to know that you have researched their school and have the ability to articulate why you want to be part of their campus community. They want specifics about how your background and interests align with their culture. Hint: this is not where you discuss how big a fan you are of their athletics or the fact that you have a lot of friends or family members who have gone there. Interviewers appreciate when students have researched specific academic programs or opportunities outside the classroom and can authentically discuss why these are interesting, exciting, and a logical match. They want you to convince them that this is one of your top choices and not simply another school on your list.

Interviewers do not want a laundry list of your activities and accomplishments. They want to discuss your motivations and goals. *Why* did you decide to start tutoring seventh graders in math after school? *Why* did you choose to run the backstage lighting for the drama club? Remember, they do not want you to get into the weeds about things like the amount of time you practiced. Instead, they want to hear about lessons learned. *What's next* now that you have seen, experienced, or discovered? This is your chance to provide context for your life in high school, to explain what you are curious about, and to give them a sense of your intentions and hopes for the future. Remember, they just want to understand who you are and what you will bring to their campus.

> **Interviewers want to know that you have researched their school and can articulate why you want to be part of their campus community.**

They do not want to ask all of the questions. Whether you are sitting down with a current student or someone who graduated 20 years ago, remember that this is someone who is not only part of a community but deeply committed to it. They are hoping to see how you will contribute and interact not only on campus as a student but also ultimately how you will represent their college as a graduate. Your responses matter but so too does your demeanor, tone, facial expressions, and body language. They do not expect every response you give to be a TED Talk. In fact, they want give and take. They want to see your personality shine through. They appreciate seeing how you respond, build on prior answers, demonstrate curiosity, and generally interact in a conversation. Interviewers make notes and later make comments in committee about students' confidence, eye contact, and engagement in the dialogue.

They want you to do well. Perhaps the biggest misconception students have—and one of the reasons they are often uneasy or nervous—is they think their interviewer is a judge who is looking to critique, find fault, and make notes of all shortcomings. This could not be further from the truth. Interviewers do understand that at age 17 or 18, this is likely one of the first interviews of your life. They are genuinely looking for sincerity and excitement about what you discuss. They enjoy when you "light up" or "nerd out" about topics, experiences, or opportunities on their campus.

We cannot tell you if you are going to be admitted to your first-choice school. We cannot tell you what to write your essay about or whether you should take a certain science class in your junior year.

What we can tell you is that at some point, the interviewer is going to look to you and ask, "What questions do you have for me?" Be ready. That is coming. What are they looking for? Interviewers want to see that you have done your homework—they almost appreciate being stumped. This is not the time to ask, "What is your mascot?" or "How many students are on campus?" When you can reference a certain professor or a specific program and ask about access you may have, where those projects or research may be going, or who else on campus is doing similar work, they make note. You can also mention a recent article from the college's student newspaper or alumni magazine and ask how the community reacted to the issue.

InitialView is a company that interviews thousands of students each year for some of the most selective colleges and universities around the world. Terry Crawford, the CEO and founder, sums it up well: "The interview is all about being able to strike the right balance: be yourself, but really that means be the mature version of yourself. Talk about and promote yourself, but don't come across as arrogant. Be humble and sound smart but don't be a know-it-all. If all that sounds both ambiguous and challenging, well, it is."

He adds,

My advice is to do what almost no one does: practice. And by prac-tice, I mean really practice your interview skills, which should involve doing a real mock interview with a stranger (perhaps a colleague of a parent or a teacher who's willing to play the role). Record the interview with your smartphone and review it along with a teacher or counselor or other adult who can give you good advice. Yes, it's awkward to see yourself on camera, but the good news is that with relatively little effort you can do something that might significantly improve your chances. The ability to connect with a stranger and get them to like you is a critical life skill—perhaps the one most critical to your future success.

What Does This Mean for You?

If a college offers an interview, we strongly encourage you to take ad-vantage of this opportunity. In fact, if the school's admission materials say "interview recommended," it should be treated as though it is required, especially if you live within an easy drive or they do regional interviews in your area. If colleges have made interviewing candidates a priority (at a significant cost of time and resources), chances are they value "demonstrated interest." If nothing else, interviewing is a useful life skill, one that will be more common as you get into college and beyond, so start now. If you are extremely nervous, try a mock interview with your school counselor or a friend of your parents. Better yet, do your first interview at a college near your home that may not be on your list. Here are a few other tips and sample questions:

Tips for Your Interview

- *Take with you:* A copy of your high school transcript to share with the interviewer (don't hesitate to talk about your course program with them); an athletic or extracurricular résumé if you have one; a portfolio if applicable; and a notebook to make notes about your impressions and to write down some questions you will ask about the college during the interview.

- *Before you go:* Talk with your parents or whoever will be accompanying you on your visit to agree upon what their role will be in the interview/visit. You, not a parent, should check in on arrival at the reception desk. When the admission officer comes out to greet you in the waiting room, be sure to introduce your family member.

- *Dress:* Institutionally appropriate—be yourself but put your best foot forward. (Be genuine and show them the best of who you are.) General things to avoid include T-shirts with slogans and names of other colleges. Don't wear clothes that are dirty or have holes. Leave your hat in the car. (These tips come from seeing all of those things and others even more ill-advised.)

- *Behavior/posture:* **Don't** flirt, slouch, put your feet on the furniture, chew gum. **Do** make eye contact, give a firm handshake before and after the interview.

- *Communication skills:* Be yourself, but be the sophisticated side of you. Avoid slang, inappropriate words, and nondescript words, such as "like," "things," "whatever," and "stuff." Conversely, do not try to impress the interviewer with SAT words that will seem too forced.

- *Modesty vs. bragging:* Don't be afraid to tell your interviewer all the wonderful things about you. Don't play down your accomplishments, but be wary of "showing off" too much. Don't try too hard; just be yourself and tell them what you are passionate about. Before you go, consider the three or four characteristics, interests, or values that you want to express to the interviewer before you leave.

- *Research:* Be sure to do your homework and research the colleges that you will visit. Do not go into a visit or interview without having read about the college and explored their website. You want the interviewer to know that you are interested enough in their school that you have taken the time to find out details about the programs, students, size, and so forth.

- *Questions:* Always have several questions you will ask the interviewer about the college. They will no doubt leave time in the interview for you to find out more about the college. (A list of potential questions is listed below.) Don't ask obvious questions that you can easily find the answer to in the viewbook or website, such as "How many students attend the college?" or "Do you have an English major?"

- *If a question stumps you:* It is perfectly acceptable to ask if you can come back to that question later after you talk some more.

- *Have fun:* Approach the interview as an opportunity to have an open conversation about who you are and what is important to you. The more relaxed you are, the better impression the interviewer will get about you as a person.

- *Follow up:* Always make sure you ask for a business card and send a thank-you note to the individual with whom you interviewed. This will go in your application file at the admission office, and it is just one more indication of your interest in the college, not to mention your superb manners!

Sample Interview Questions

- What is the most significant contribution you have made to your school?

- If I visited your school, what would I find is your role in the school community?

- What would your teachers say are your greatest strengths as a person and as a student?

- What is one thing you would change about your high school?

- What do you like about your high school?

- What might you study in college?

- What courses have you taken? Why?

- What has been your favorite subject in high school? Why?

- What books did you read last summer? Do you have a favorite and why?

- What three adjectives would your friends use to describe you?

- What are some of your personal and career goals for the future?

- What kind of development do you hope to see in yourself in the next four years?

- What do you enjoy doing in your free time?

- How have you spent your summers?

- How would you describe yourself as a person?

- What events would you say have been crucial to your life thus far? People?

- Do you have any heroes?

- Are you satisfied with your accomplishments and growth thus far?

- Why are you interested in our school?

- What do you think you will contribute to this college environment?

- Have you ever thought of not going to college right away? What would you do?

- If you could talk to any one person past or present, to whom would you talk? Why?

- Where and when do you find yourself stimulated intellectually?

- What is one activity you are involved in extracurricularly and why?

Questions You Can Ask

- What are the most important campus issues to students at this college?

- What are the greatest strengths of the college?

- What would you change about the school?

- How does the admission office judge whether a student is a good fit?

- What is the college's retention rate? Why do students decide to transfer out?

- How safe is the college campus?

- What do students do on weekends? Where does most of the social life take place?

- According to students, what is the most difficult course offered on campus?

- How is this college trying to improve itself?

- How close are the students and faculty here?

- How has this college changed in the last five years?

LETTERS OF RECOMMENDATION

Note: The current student-to-counselor ratio in the United States is nearly 500:1. (This is double the ratio recommended by the National Association for College Admission Counseling.) As on all other sections of your application, admission readers do understand your context and environment. Readers do understand that in extremely large high schools your time with counselors or teachers is limited. If you are in a high school like that, be assured that committees will not hold a generic or brief letter of recommendation against you in their review.

On your application, your personal details (hometown, family information, etc.) provide a *sketch* of your background. Grades, classes, and test scores *outline* your academic ability. Extracurricular involvement and writing *provide color by filling in details* about what you love or how you think and approach life or where you want to go in the future. Letters from counselors and teachers in your school are the *frame* for the picture you have painted—they support you by complementing and enhancing your application. While we understand that you will not be the one writing your letters of recommendation, these are a significant component of the application, and it is important for you to have a sense of what readers and committees are expecting as they review letters of recommendation.

Whose Letters Do Colleges Want to Read?

Colleges *do* want to hear from teachers or counselors or other community members who are excited about what you have to offer. Effective recommendation letters reinforce character traits and patterns of behavior that you have likely alluded to already in your application. Readers want to understand the role you play in class, the way you approach problems, your level of self-awareness, and the impact you have had on your team or club or fellow employees. They read recommendations and ask if that characterization aligns with their campus ethos and dynamic. In chapter 1, you thought through why you were going to college. Help your recommenders out by sharing your answers, as well as how that has led you to apply to specific schools.

> Effective recommendation letters reinforce character traits and patterns of behavior that you have already alluded to in your application.

Colleges *do* value an enthusiastic advocate who will provide an invaluable perspective that puts you in the context of your school, your class, and the other students they have taught during their career. Ideally, admission officers want someone who has seen you grow, change, improve, and learn, even if along the way you had struggles and doubts. This means that you do not need to choose the teacher in whose class you had the highest grade or the coach who saw you shoot the winning basket to win the state championship. Often, in fact, the recommendation letters that are the least persuasive are those that make you seem perfect. You are not. Readers know this and do not expect it. They want real. They want authentic. They want someone who knows your weaknesses and difficulties and yet is so excited about your potential that they cannot wait to write on your behalf.

Colleges *do* appreciate someone who can add something new. "Johnny is a caring, charismatic, and courageous student. He has a 4.0 GPA and a 34 on the ACT. He is involved in X, Y, and Z activities. He would make a great addition to your campus. The end." While all of these characteristics may be true, admission readers have seen this information somewhere else in the application. Compelling letters bring a new angle. Sometimes they are surprising and make readers say or think, "Really? I never would have expected that." They want to hear from an insider.

Whose Letters Do Colleges Not Want to Read?

Colleges *do not* need to hear from someone who taught or coached you in middle school. Recommendation letters are included in order to provide depth and insight. Unfortunately, every year admission officers receive letters from teachers, coaches, club sponsors, or band directors who are unable to provide recent, relevant, compelling insight. Do not waste the opportunity to have someone "frame" the portrait you have painted with outdated or extremely limited knowledge of your character and potential.

Colleges *do not* care about big titles. Every year admission offices receive letters from senators, actors, and athletes. Often these come with pictures, which can be fun. They will get posted on the back of doors or passed around the office. However, normally these are recycled form letters that they have seen year after year and add no real value. If a college asks for a recommendation from someone other than a counselor or teacher, they would rather hear from your neighbor who has watched you grow up, whose kids you have babysat for the last three years, and who is as proud of you as your own parents than someone with a recognizable name, face, or title.

What Does This Mean for You?

Consider the voices that have emerged in your application. You have listed your family background, your classes, honors, and activities and written an essay that tells a story about who you are. Your school counselor will write a recommendation on behalf of the school elaborating your role in, and contributions to, the community. Perhaps you have interviewed and provided context for your high school experience in the additional information section. When you are choosing teachers to write recommendations in support of your application, determine what has not been communicated and allow that to guide you. Has your perseverance not come to light as you might have hoped? If so, ask a teacher who saw you struggle with a subject and double down to overcome the challenge. Students fall into the trap of simply asking the teachers who gave them the best grades. Most students will ask two teachers for recommendations (some colleges require two but others limit submission to one), so balance the voices speaking on your behalf. You might be a humanities student, but sending recommendations from two English teachers will be redundant. Consider asking a math/science teacher who can talk about the right side of your brain.

Teacher recommendations are just that, from teachers who have worked with you in the classroom (ideally in junior or senior year). Admission officers do not want that teacher to go into your extracurricular involvement. They want to know who you are as a learner, classmate, lab partner, and so on. Choose a teacher who will speak to your creativity, curiosity, and ability to think analytically, synthesize material, and write fluidly.

"What if they don't write me a good recommendation?" This is a question we often hear, and the answer is simple. If there is any reason to think they wouldn't write well about you, ask someone else. In fact, it is perfectly acceptable to say to a teacher, "I would really appreciate if you would write on my behalf, and I am curious if you think you know me well enough to write a positive recommendation." If they cannot, they will decline. (It is not like they need more work.)

You should give your counselor, teacher, or other recommenders several weeks' notice before the deadline. Go to them well in advance to have a conversation. Ask them if they are willing to write for you. Go through the points we highlighted above. Be honest about what you are hoping they can offer as a supporter, an advocate, an insider, a frame.

:💡: *Try This*

This chapter is full of exercises for you to try. Spend some time going back through it, and make an activities list, do some creative writing, discuss interview questions with a friend or family member, and brainstorm about recommenders. Starting these now will avoid the last-minute scramble as deadlines approach.

💬 **Talk About This**

1. What are your primary takeaways about how admission readers are considering your nonacademic information and background?

2. How might your essay or short-answer responses differ among the colleges you plan to apply to?

3. Does understanding more about what colleges are looking for outside the classroom help you remove or add any specific colleges to your list?

👍 **CHECK IN** After reading this chapter, are you still on the same page? If you are not all-in together, what do you need to do, discuss, or learn to get there?

CHAPTER 8

Admission Decisions

Why do we never get an answer / When we are knocking
at the door / Because the truth is hard to swallow /
That's what the war of love is for.
"QUESTION" BY THE MOODY BLUES

Kaffee: Colonel Jessep, did you order the Code Red?

Col. Jessep: You want answers?

Kaffee: I think I'm entitled to.

Col. Jessep: You want answers?

Kaffee: I want the truth!

Col. Jessep: You can't handle the truth!

In this famous scene from the movie *A Few Good Men*, Lt. Kaffee (Tom
Cruise), a young, somewhat naive navy lawyer, cross-examines the
highly decorated, deeply respected Col. Jessep (Jack Nicholson). He is
attempting to determine whether the colonel ordered a "Code Red"—a
covert order that allegedly led to the death of an enlisted Marine. As
you can tell, Jessep genuinely does not think Kaffee or any nonofficer
can truly comprehend the factors and pressures that surround his role
and actions. Now, college admission is not the Marines, but the scene
and quote are still fitting as we head into this chapter.

HERE IS WHAT YOU KNOW

You now have a more accurate portrait of the higher-education landscape. You know there are thousands of colleges and universities in our nation. You know there are great colleges abroad and more Americans going overseas for college than ever before, so you are not even limited to staying in this country once you finish high school—the landscape is indeed global, and the options are vast. You know that most institutions are admitting more students than they deny and many are utilizing academic criteria only to make admission decisions. They are operating in a very outward-facing, transparent, formulaic manner.

You know that the first principle of college admission is the same as microeconomics—supply and demand. The number of applications for the number of spots in the class drives admit rate. If quality and number continue to go up, selectivity also goes up, and therefore admit rate goes down. Lastly, you know that when the quality and number of applicants to a particular college increases, schools add factors to their admission process. They often begin to operate in a holistic process and incorporate far more than grades and test scores.

In chapters 6 and 7, we offered you a peek behind the curtain. You now understand what these colleges are looking for and the conversations that are occurring in committees. That information, insight, and knowledge will help you as you apply to colleges and consider how one varies from another in their priorities and goals.

Now you have arrived at the "courtroom" chapter—*how* admission decisions are actually made and why. What? You thought we already covered that? The real question is, "Can you handle the truth?"

THE TRUTH

First—and this is elementary but important—holistic review means it is a human process. Human means subjective. Human, we can all agree, means imperfect. Human means unpredictable. Feeling better?

Second, they are making increasingly nuanced decisions with limited information in a compressed amount of time. Still not feeling better?

Third, they are often moving very quickly past the quantitative factors (test scores and grades) because of the high academic quality of their applicants.

Undeniably, there is something hardwired in all of us that longs for right, equal, and just—a perfect process and predictable results. In college admission, *the truth* is that imperfect humans, operating in sub-optimal conditions, are reviewing extremely qualitative and personal information (your writing, your background, your experiences, your interests, and your strengths) and comparing them, in a relative manner, to thousands of others. So, in addition to not being perfect or predictable, holistic admission *is not fair*.

Therefore, it is no surprise that these are the refrains we hear each year.

> "How can you wait list my son? He has 30 points higher and two more AP classes than your average. And we know someone down the street who got in that . . ."

> "Something is wrong with your process if my daughter who has been through as many medical issues as she has and still has a 3.8 is not getting in. Talk about not being fair."

> "And don't get me started on financial aid—or lack thereof. Talk about an injustice."

It may surprise you to hear that our admission colleagues around the country who work for colleges that annually deny admission to thousands of incredibly talented students are shaking their heads right along with you. They would not contest your very rational responses and perspective. You are not crazy. They know. They agree. It is *not* fair. In fact, they would be the first to concur that they deny many students with higher SAT/ACT scores or more community service or a stronger curriculum or who wrote better essays or participated in more clubs and sports than other applicants who were admitted.

Take some time to speak with a student or a family who applied to selective colleges recently. Go talk to a counselor or a teacher in your school who sees entire classes of students receive admission decisions on an annual basis. You will likely hear them relay anecdotes like the one about the student with the perfect test scores who was not admitted; the three-sport athlete who also volunteers at the hospital who was deferred, wait-listed, and ultimately denied; or the one about the double legacy whose grandfather also taught at the institution who did not get in.

> Holistic admission is absolutely not *fair*, but it seeks to be consistent.

If you are looking for fair, you have come to the wrong place. Holistic admission is absolutely not that, but it seeks to be consistent.

INSTITUTIONAL MISSION

Supply and demand (the number of applications for the number of seats available in a class) is the first principle of college admission. Fulfilling institutional mission is the second—and there are only two. Be it Northwestern University or Northeastern University, University of Washington or Washington University, Reed College or Wright State University, they all have a motto, as well as a vision and mission statement. In other words, each school was founded and continues to exist for a specific reason. The type of students they are attempting to recruit and enroll is specific, and their admission process will support that. Therefore, the goal of admission deans, directors, and vice presidents around the country is *not* to be fair; it is *not* to be able to publish a formula for families to use to predict their chances of being admitted. Instead, it is to advance their institution's mission.

Mission Drives Admission

Mission means that middle-50-percent test and grade ranges or averages that you see posted on websites or in publications are *guides, not guarantees*. They are only a small part of the much bigger story. Mission means that rigor of curriculum, course performance, impact on your community, essays, recommendations from teachers and counselors, interviews all matter, but they are not the only factors at play.

Look at the academic profiles of Amherst and Caltech, and you will find they are quite similar in test score ranges. But take a look at their missions:

Amherst College

Terras Irradient *"Let Them Give Light to the World"*

Amherst College educates men and women of exceptional potential from all backgrounds so that they may seek, value, and advance knowledge, engage the world around them, and lead principled lives of consequence.

Amherst brings together the most promising students, whatever their financial need, in order to promote diversity of experience and ideas within a purposefully small residential community. Working with faculty, staff, and administrators dedicated to intellectual freedom and the highest standards of instruction in the liberal arts, Amherst undergraduates assume substantial responsibility for undertaking inquiry and for shaping their education within and beyond the curriculum.

Amherst College is committed to learning through close colloquy and to expanding the realm of knowledge through scholarly research and artistic creation at the highest level. Its graduates link learning with leadership—in service to the College, to their communities, and to the world beyond. (Amherst College 2018)

California Institute of Technology

The mission of the California Institute of Technology is to expand human knowledge and benefit society through research integrated with education. We investigate the most challenging, fundamental problems in science and technology in a singularly collegial, interdisciplinary atmosphere, while educating outstanding students to become creative members of society. (Caltech 2018)

The difference in school mission is why it is possible for a student to be admitted to a school with a higher rank or lower admit rate than another college to which they are denied. The student applying to Amherst (same profile, involvement, writing ability, scores, and grades) is going to be read and discussed through a completely different lens than they will at Caltech. Mission, at least in part, is what counselors are talking about when they discuss fit or match.

Geography—particularly at selective, public universities—is one driver that can dictate admission decisions. The University of North

Geography—particularly at selective, public universities—is one driver that can dictate admission decisions.

Carolina system is mandated by their legislature to enroll no more than 18 percent of students from outside of the state (Pennington 2016). This is why the admit rate for UNC–Chapel Hill is typically more than three times higher for in-state students than nonresidents.

The University of North Carolina at Chapel Hill

The nation's first public university, serves North Carolina, the United States, and the world through teaching, research, and public service. We embrace an unwavering commitment to excellence as one of the world's great research universities.

Our mission is to serve as a center for research, scholarship, and creativity and to teach a diverse community of undergraduate, graduate, and professional students to become the next generation of leaders. Through the efforts of our exceptional faculty and staff, and with generous support from North Carolina's citizens, we invest our knowledge and resources to enhance access to learning and to foster the success and prosperity of each rising generation. We also extend knowledge-based services and other resources of the University to the citizens of North Carolina and their institutions to enhance the quality of life for all people in the State. (University of North Carolina–Chapel Hill 2018)

Every year, there are valedictorians from other states around the country who are not admitted to UNC–Chapel Hill but are accepted by Ivy League schools. Does this sound controversial or unfair? Not if you understand that *mission drives admission.* A college closes their nursing program; they begin offering majors in engineering; they eliminate their wrestling team; they build a new residence hall and increase the size of their first-year class. Mission changes, and with it admission decisions are altered to support those goals.

A Quick Look at Georgia Tech

Founded in 1885, classes began in 1888 with one major—mechanical engineering. At the time, it was an all-male trade school responding to the needs of nineteenth- and early-twentieth-century Georgia and the

US South. The focus was on training and preparing young men for industry, leadership, and imagining and creating new products and advancements in a rapidly industrializing state, region, and nation. Were there more "qualified" or "smarter" students at the time who had aspirations of becoming ministers or lawyers or physicians? Unquestionably. Had they applied with those intentions, they likely would not have been admitted. It was not Tech's mission to educate students for those roles.

In 1912, Georgia Tech established a School of Commerce, which functioned as their business program. In 1952, Tech opened its doors to women for the first time and in 1961 became the first school in the South to integrate classes without a court order. Imagine a family who had two boys. One started Tech in 1950. Three years later, the younger brother applies. He is by all accounts smarter than his older brother but ultimately not admitted. A shift in mission changed the applicant pool, the admission process, and the competition. Supply and demand drive admit rates. If supply grows, due to a shift in mission, then admission decisions also change based on factors outside of the ones we covered in chapters 6 and 7.

Georgia Tech

Technological change is fundamental to the advancement of the human condition. The Georgia Tech community—students, staff, faculty, and alumni—will realize our motto of "Progress and Service" through effectiveness and innovation in teaching and learning, our research advances, and entrepreneurship in all sectors of society. We will be leaders in improving the human condition in Georgia, the United States, and around the globe. (Georgia Institute of Technology 2018)

Can you pick up on institutional priorities and start to imagine the rubrics for review? It is not hard to hear conversations in the admission committee that focus on identifying students who have established a commitment to or show potential for "improving the human condition" or who demonstrate evidence of "Progress and Service."

Reading the mission statements, you can predict priorities and likely infer how geography, major, background,

Reading the mission statements, you can predict priorities.

and so forth will affect and influence conversations in admission committees that contribute to decisions.

An Olympic Example

In the 2016 Summer Olympics, Gabby Douglas (the defending gold medalist from 2012) competed in the women's gymnastics all-around qualifying round. After four events (vault, uneven bars, balance beam, and floor exercise), she finished third out of the 24 competitors (top 12 percent). Sounds pretty good, right? However, in this humanly judged competition, she was eliminated, because the rules state that only the top two finishers from each country are able to advance to the next round. In this case, she was third overall (by one-fourth of a point) but also third among Americans. That is right—the top two competitors were Simone Biles and Aly Raisman—two of her US teammates.

Sound familiar? She was competing in an incredibly talented pool, in a very specific year, in a competition with particular rules, judged by imperfect humans making slight calculations over multiple factors (events). Fair? No. Perfect? No. Reality? Yes.

Here is the thing though—she signed up for it. Gabby knew this was not a preset bar that all she had to do was jump over. Would she have lost a night's sleep before performing at a local or state-level competition? Absolutely not. She could have stayed out late the night before eating Cheetos and still waltzed in and cruised to first place. But on that stage—with that competition—she understood that advancing was not guaranteed.

CAN YOU HANDLE THE TRUTH?

Gabby's margin was 12 percent. Only a handful of colleges in our nation have admit rates of 12 percent or less. If you are applying to one of these—and frankly, if you are applying to a school taking less than 50 percent—you need to understand that getting edged out for reasons you may never know is a distinct possibility. There is not going to be a check box on the application that asks you to acknowledge this, but perhaps there should be. You may be among the best in your high school, county, or even state, but that does not guarantee you will be selected from such a deep and talented pool of applicants in a process driven by institutional priorities and a specific mission. You may have 18 relatives who have attended that university. You may have been wearing that school's gear since you were in diapers. You may have aced all of your AP tests and the math section of the ACT. But in that year, for that college, and based on where you're from, what you want to study, what that university is emphasizing or deemphasizing (institutional priorities), and—most importantly—the rest of the competition, you may not get admitted.

HANDLING THOSE ADMISSION DECISIONS

We believe you can handle the truth. We believe that, as a family, your focus is now not simply getting in but staying together through the college admission experience. We have walked you through how decisions are really made. Now it is time to understand the possible admission decision scenarios—and how to handle them.

Defer

Each year many students are "deferred" from the Early Action (EA) or Early Decision (ED) round to Regular Decision (RD). Essentially, this is a college's way of hedging their bets. They are going to admit the students who the admission staff are 100 percent confident about wanting to enroll, deny the students they are 100 percent confident are not academically competitive or are not good matches for their institution, and then defer the rest. They want to get a sense of the strength and size of their entire applicant pool once regular decision applications are submitted and not overextend their offers early. It is common to see 20 to 40 percent of EA/ED applicants deferred to the next round.

What Does This Mean for You?

It means you have some work to do. You will need to send in your final fall grades. You may need to write an additional essay or submit a form telling the admission committee more about your senior-year extracurricular activities. Defer is a "hold on" or a "tell us more." They will be looking at how you have done in a challenging senior schedule or if your upward grade trend will continue or if you can juggle more responsibility outside the classroom with your course load. Use the deferral to refocus and motivate you to finish your senior year well. It might even mean retaking standardized tests to try and score closer to their admitted-student profile.

It means you may need to submit another application or two. The good news is that many great schools have deadlines in January, after most EA/ED decisions are released. Bottom line—you need applications in at a few schools with higher admit rates and lower academic profiles than the one that deferred you.

It means holistic review is a real thing. Whether your scores and grades were above, below, or directly in the middle of their academic profile, a defer only proves what you already knew—admission is about more than numbers. Institutional priorities, shaping a class, and supply and demand drive admission decisions. Remember, you signed up for this.

It means you need to check your ego and wait. We told you college admission was not designed to be fair—now you are living that reality. Unfortunately, defer means spending a few more months in limbo. The committee has decided they want to evaluate you in the context of their overall pool. Do not let your ego get in your way. Too many students do not send in fall grades, complete the deferred form, or send other information schools ask for because their pride is shaken. Think of the admission experience as your first foray into your college years, and start looking at *maybes* as good things. There will be many more to come. They call it an admission *process* for a reason—it is not always over in one round. Do not go halfway and stop.

It means you need to look forward, not backward. If you are deferred, *do not* look back. *Do not* second-guess whether you should have taken AP Geography in the ninth grade instead of band or blame Mr. Thompson for giving you an 89 instead of a 93 that would have bumped your GPA by .00083. Control what you can control. Are you going to get admitted in the next round? Maybe. You need to control what you can control. You only get one senior year. Do well—but more importantly do good. Do not worry about admission offices you will never enter, but recommit to the rooms you walk into every day. Be a good friend. Be a good sibling. Be a good teammate. Go thank a teacher who wrote a recommendation for you. Hug your parents.

Wait List

Otherwise known as admission purgatory, there is no other way to say it—the wait list sucks. Go ahead and add this to your running list of other "things that suck," along with pink eye, losing to your biggest rival in the final seconds, and someone leaving an empty box of Girl Scout cookies in the pantry. You have already waited for a decision (sometimes having already been deferred), and now you are being asked to wait again.

Why Do Schools Have a Wait List?

It depends whom you ask. Deans, directors, and other enrollment managers will say it is because predicting 17-year-old behavior is not an exact science. Parents and students will say it is because enrollment people are not that smart or maybe even a little cruel. After all, if colleges could predict *exactly* how many students each year would accept their offer of admission (i.e., "yield") and deposit by the May 1 National Candidate Reply Deadline, wait lists would not be necessary. Perhaps one day we will live in a world where students only apply to one college; all get admitted, enroll, are happy, earn 4.0 GPAs, retain at 100 percent, graduate in four years, get high-paying and fulfilling jobs after graduation, name their babies after the admission director, and then donate consistently and generously for the rest of their lives. Until that time, we have wait lists.

Colleges build and utilize historical yield models to predict the number of students who will say yes to their offer. However, because the number of beds in residence halls, the number of seats in classrooms, and the faculty-to-student or advisor-to-student ratios are very specific, they intentionally plan to come in slightly below their target. They do this to account for the years when the model changes and students "over-yield." If you are applying to a school that overenrolled the year prior, you can be sure that they will be extremely conservative—that is, fill an even higher number of spaces from their wait list.

The wait list also exists to allow schools to meet institutional priorities. After the May 1 deposit deadline, colleges evaluate their deposited class and then use their wait list to accommodate for demographics that were not met in the initial round of admission offers. They may want more students from a particular state or geographic region to

> The wait list exists in part to allow schools to meet institutional priorities.

proliferate their college's brand. They may have just hired a new dean in business who is clamoring to grow the program. Maybe they are still trying to find those female chemistry students who we learned about in chapter 2. Ultimately, students chosen from the wait list are handpicked to fill a specific purpose: net tuition revenue, academic profile, academic major, and so on.

What Does This Mean for You?

It means you need to accept your spot. At most schools the wait list decision is actually an offer. Check what they send you, and read their website closely. Typically, you need to take action of some kind to accept or claim your wait list spot. Alternatively, you can decide to close or cancel your application for continued consideration.

If you do claim your spot, be sure you do anything additional that they instruct. Is there a supplementary short-answer question they want you to complete? Do they want you to send another recommendation letter or schedule an interview? Each school will handle this differently, so read your letter, email, or online information carefully.

It means you need to deposit at another college. The university that has offered you a spot on their wait list should be instructing you to take this step, but this is absolutely critical. Because most schools won't have a firm sense of deposits until late April, the majority of wait list activity occurs in May and June. Since May 1 is the National Candidate Reply Deadline, you need to put your money down at another college in order to secure your spot in their class. Just like the college, you are hedging your bets. Additionally, you should assume that you will not be pulled from the wait list and begin to get excited about the school that accepted you and where you have chosen to deposit.

It means you should reach out to your admission counselor (unless they specifically tell you not to). If you have met or corresponded with someone from the admission office, perhaps when they visited your high school or while you were on their campus, send them an email. Let them know you claimed your spot on the wait list and completed the school's stipulated form or essay. You are indicating continued interest in attending. If they end up going to their wait list, it is not going to be ranked. Wait list activity is all about shaping a class—and you want to be at the top of their mind. To be clear, we are not telling you to reach out every day. This is a one-and-done proposition. We have seen students send a painted shoe with a message on the bottom reading: "just trying to get my foot in the door." Memorable, but ultimately ineffective. Admission offices regularly receive chocolates, cookies, and other treats along with poems or notes. It is safe to say that a couple hundred grams of sugar and a few couplets are not going to outweigh institutional priorities. There is a distinct line between demonstrating interest and stalking. Stay in your lane.

It means you need to wait well. Waiting is not easy. Uncertainty is frustrating and unsettling. We do not have a solution for that. What we can tell you is that life is full of situations like this. Will I get a new job and when? Will a house come on the market that we can afford in the area we want to live in? Will the results of this test come back from the doctor with life-changing implications? This may be the first time you have had to wait for something you really wanted—to have to sit in a period of uncertainty—but it will not be the last. This can be particularly hard because it seems like everyone else is all set and everything is smooth. Trust us: other people always seem like they have it together. Life looks easy for them (especially if you believe their social media account). Your goal is to have the confidence to embrace uncertainty as an adventure rather than a burden. Do not let being in limbo keep you from enjoying the last part of your senior year. Have fun on spring break. Go to prom. Take the opportunity to thank your teachers or read something outside of school in which you are genuinely interested. Being content and joyful in the present is a challenge at any age. You are just getting some early practice.

> Your goal is to have the confidence to embrace uncertainty as an adventure rather than a burden.

Deny

As a strong student and an achiever, this very well may be one of the first "nos" you have heard. It is never easy or fun. We were both denied by colleges. We have had girlfriends break up with us. We have been turned down for jobs. Your goal is to look at a deny not as a hard stop but rather as a pivot.

What Does This Mean for You?

It means you are not OK. Go ahead and scream, cry, beat your pillow, cook or eat a lot of something. (Do all of those at once if you're really upset.) Whatever it takes to begin clearing your head. Mad? Sad? Frustrated? Disappointed? All of these are totally valid. Give yourself the time, space, and permission to process those very real thoughts and feelings.

It means you will be OK. When you are denied admission, you need to remember that no college (or person or job or car or city) is perfect. Perfect colleges do not exist—a perfect mentality does. This *is* going to work out. Here is how we know: every year—*every year*—we talk to current college students who say they did not end up at their first choice because they were denied, and they are so glad. They cannot imagine being anywhere but the place they landed. In the days immediately after a denial you will not believe that, but it is 100 percent true. Fact: you are going to end up somewhere great.

Jim Bock, the vice president and dean of admission at Swarthmore College, explains,

—

There is no perfect student or perfect school and most students would be successful at multiple institutions. I have always argued that students should have several "first" choices as they navigate the admissions process, and given the breadth and depth of choice and opportunity in this country, a less than desirable outcome from one school is really that school's loss and another school's gain. There is a place, multiple places I believe, for every student. This one decision does not and should not define you. Some might say that's easy for me to say given where I sit today, but I have personal experience. I was deferred, then denied early action at my first choice college over thirty years ago, and it made all of the difference. I added a few schools to my list, including Swarthmore, and it changed my life forever. It's part of why I do what I do today. I was disappointed, but it made me more hungry and made me rethink my options and look past the bad tour or less compelling group session and really focus on what set each school apart from one another.

—

It means college admission is not fair. As our colleague Pam Ambler from Pace Academy in Atlanta says, "The way that admission decisions *feel* is not how they are *made*." That is spot-on advice. If someone breaks up with you and says, "It's not you, it's me," they are lying. It *is* you. But for colleges it is about *them*: institutional mission, supply and demand, and Gabby Douglas. You know this.

Gary Clark, the director of undergraduate admission at UCLA, advises students, "Remember that there are two names on every diploma. One, the institution's, the other, the student's. While you may picture yourself at one university, remember that there are many that could offer you a wonderful experience. If it doesn't work out at your top choice, and you've developed a strong list of prospective universities, then you rally around one of those other options and get excited about the experience you'll have there."

Translation: You may get denied by a school based on where you are from or what you want to study or because they are trying to grow this or that and you happen to be that and this. It is fine to *feel* disappointed or mad or upset. Just be sure you do not equate this decision to an indictment of your character or a prediction of your future success or potential.

It means you need to be realistic and move on. If you are denied in early action or early decision, then, like a deferral, you will need to submit a few more applications to schools with higher admit rates and lower academic profiles (i.e., "target" and "likely" schools) than the one that denied you. If you are denied in regular decision, go back to class and finish the year well, because the colleges that ultimately admit you will be looking closely at your final high school transcript to insure you did not have any academic issues after you received their decision.

Technically, you do have the ability to appeal your admission decision. The truth is almost none of these are successful. You can likely find a college's appeal form and process on their website. If you appeal, be sure to read the conditions of a "reasonable appeal." While each school is different, typically valid reasons include not having your correct transcript or receiving inaccurate or incomplete grading information. Major medical situations or severe life circumstances you neglected to include in your application may also be considered. "Really wanting to go" or because that was the only place to which you applied or because everyone in your family has gone there—not valid.

One of our colleagues puts it this way: "If you decide to appeal, you need to be prepared to be denied again." Damn. That sounds cold. The truth is like that sometimes. Actually, the truth is like that a lot.

Get back to your classes, your team, your job, your clubs, and your family. Take some time to look around at practice or over the holiday break at the relationships you have built. Be reminded of the community you created and the bonds, closeness, and sense of belonging you feel. They want you with them. They love having you as part of it all—and other colleges are going to invite you into similar communities.

Parents, What Does This Mean for You?

You love your kids. We started with that in chapter 1. The topic may be the college admission experience, but the theme is love and family. When admission decisions like defer, wait list, and deny come, it hurts. Just like we said earlier, you also are going to likely *feel* mad, sad, frustrated, and disappointed. Again, all of these are totally valid. The difference is that you cannot scream and beat your pillow. (Totally fine, however, to eat or cook a lot of something.)

It means you have some work to do before decisions are released. If your student is applying to a selective college, you need to prepare them for "no"—and also for *maybe* (i.e., defer and wait list). You understand the statistics. You understand the driving factors behind admission decisions. You know that Gabby Douglas was one of the world's best gymnasts in 2016 and easily could have advanced to the women's all-around finals. The reality is that you will not know and cannot control admission decisions. In the weeks leading up to these decisions being released, we are encouraging you to spend one of your weekly college meetings talking about that. Be sure your daughter or son hears you say again that these decisions have no correlation to how much you love them and believe in them. Encourage them and remind them that not getting into a certain college has absolutely no bearing on their future success or potential.

It means you have some work to do on the day decisions are released. The good news is that when decisions come out, you just need to do the same thing you have done their entire lives—be available. Like the decisions themselves, you will not know the emotions or reactions that are coming: door slamming, dead silence, screaming, crying. Any of these are possible. Nobody ever said adulting was easy—and here is another test. On this day, it will not be about words but simply about being there.

We have heard of families who have planned to go to a movie or cook a favorite meal or who have bought a certain ice cream in advance. Sometimes this is exactly what they will want and need after the decision comes out, and other times you will need to read the moment and call an audible. In other words, parenting. You got this.

It means you have some work to do after decisions are released. In the days and weeks following one of these decisions, your job is to refocus and encourage. As we said earlier, if your student receives a deny or defer decision in early action or early decision, it will likely mean submitting a few more applications and sending in final fall semester grades. Find appropriate times to help them maintain focus on keeping their grades up as all colleges will be looking at those to make final decisions. Help them look forward to next steps and the possibilities of what is to come rather than bemoaning or questioning a decision that has already been made and issued. Keep preaching the bigger picture and emphasizing that this is their one and only senior year. Continue to be their biggest cheerleader. Remind them that they are going to have some great college options and that you are excited to see how it all plays out.

> Parents, after a denial, remind students that they will have some great college options and that you are excited to see how it all plays out.

Admit

What, you think we forgot? Absolutely not. We were just saving the good news for last. You would think that there is not much here to explain, but, almost comically, we get calls from students every year saying, "So . . . I logged into my portal, and it says that I have been accepted. Does that mean I'm in?" I guess some folks still like to hear it the old-fashioned way. We can do that: *"Congratulations!"*

What Does This Mean for You?

It means you need to celebrate. Celebrate every admit. Go out to dinner, buy something you have been wanting for a while, or just go get a double scoop of ice cream—whatever makes you happy. Be proud! Take some time to look back on all of the hard work it has taken to get to this point, and be thankful there is a community out there that not only recognizes that but also thinks you could come to their campus and make it better. That's pretty awesome, right?

It means you need to be cool. Keep in mind two things: (1) That could have easily broken the other way for you, especially if it was a highly selective college. We are not suggesting that you are not amazing, but holistic admission is unpredictable, as we have discussed. (2) Some crazy qualified and talented students did *not* get in, and they are disappointed and hurting. Act like you have been there before. Keep it classy. There is a big difference between "Wow. I was accepted to Michigan. So honored to have the chance to go there" and "Got into Michigan today. They would have been crazy not to take me" (a.k.a. the *opposite* of being cool). The schools who admit you are excited for you to join their community because you have been a positive influencer in yours. Be cognizant of your classmates, friends, and others who got some disappointing news recently. A little humility goes a long way.

It means you need to read the entire letter. The first paragraph will inevitably be filled with congratulatory language, accolades, and perhaps a transition to starting to convince you about why you should choose that school. Somewhere, however, perhaps even in a bolded or underlined section, they will outline their expectations for your continued demonstration of both strong academic performance and good citizenship. They are basically saying, "Don't screw this up." They expect you to keep focused on your grades and to let them know in advance if you are considering a schedule change that diverges from what you told them on your application. They expect you to not be suspended, expelled, or arrested. As you read this, it may sound funny or ridiculous. Trust us—all of that language is in there because of prior student behavior. You have worked hard to earn these offers of admission. Don't blow it.

It means you are going to have a decision to make. By the May 1 National Candidate Reply Deadline you will need to put down your enrollment deposit *at only one school*. Deposit amounts vary widely and will all be outlined in your acceptance letter and subsequent emails or correspondence. In chapter 9, we are going to give you some ways to weigh and consider your options. For now—go back to celebrating!

 Try This

Take the Admission Decision Pledge

All: I, [state your name], being of sound (though overly caffeinated) mind and (sleep-deprived) body, do hereby swear that I will *not* presume anything in the admission process.

Students: Upon advice of these author sages, I acknowledge that when looking at middle-50-percent ranges, I will *not* expect that my test scores, though in the top quartile, guarantee my admittance. I will *not* look at middle-50-percent ranges of hitherto admitted classes and expect my scores, though in the bottom quartile, will be overlooked based on my amazing essay, pictures of me in a onesie from that college, or the 12 letters of recommendation that have been sent on my behalf.

Parents: Henceforth, I vow to utilize singular-case pronouns when referring to future college hopes and dreams. I hereby attest that I will not attempt to emulate the voice of an adolescent in order to obtain the password to an account or a decision in advance through covert and clandestine measures. I attest that I will *not* begrudge the joy and excitement of my friends when their children receive positive results.

All: I understand the heretofore explicated concept of holistic admission is neither fair nor perfect, wherein I will likely not agree with nor be capable of predicting all results, despite the complex algorithms I employ or the kingdom fortune-tellers I visit.

Parents: Furthermore, I agree that I will *not* view an admission decision as a referendum on or a cumulative assessment of my parental faculties.

Students: Furthermore, I agree that I will *not* view an admission decision as an indictment of my character, a judgment on my hitherto demonstrated preparation, nor a prediction of my future success.

Note: slightly misused Olde English conjunctions do not negate the spirit nor effectiveness of this pledge.

💬 Talk About This

1. How do the mission statements of the colleges you are considering align with your values and aspirations?

2. How can your family prepare for the different decisions you may receive?

3. What truth about college admission decisions encourages and concerns you the most?

👍 **CHECK IN** After reading this chapter, are you still on the same page? If you're not all-in together, what do you need to do, discuss, or learn to get there?

PART IV

CHAPTER 9

Making Your College Choice

Burn the ships, cut the ties / Send a flare into the night /
Say a prayer, turn the tide.
"BURN THE SHIPS" BY KING AND COUNTRY

It is all about the vibe . . . oh, and the money
HIGH SCHOOL SENIOR

May your choices reflect your hopes not your fears.
NELSON MANDELA

Once you make a decision, the universe conspires to make it happen.
RALPH WALDO EMERSON

Despite a decade of parenting, I (Brennan) recently made a rookie mistake. I took my son into our local candy shop, and with the sweet aroma of fresh chocolate and sugar taunting his senses, I allowed him to choose a treat. He was paralyzed. "I don't know how to decide," he said—his initial excitement quickly besieged by choice.

I immediately recognized the puzzled look of wonder on his face, as it resembled those of the high school seniors I counsel each year. After spending months in anticipation waiting for colleges to make their decisions, acceptances roll in, and the tables are turned. We are confident that if you follow our guidance, you will have a handful of college acceptances from schools where you could see yourself thriving.

Like a kid in a candy shop, you will have to choose. For many students, this will be the most significant decision they have made to this point, and it is a complicated one. Selecting a college involves choosing a new home, reestablishing friends and community, and making a major financial decision all rolled into one. Too often, students and families experience the type of anxiety that the author and psychologist Barry Schwartz points out in his book *Paradox of Choice: Why More Is Less*. In the spring, after the admission deposit is submitted, or during summer at orientation, or even as the fall semester begins, we commonly hear students express lingering doubt and uncertainty about their selection. Our goal is to provide you with the tools and questions that you need to appreciate the privilege you have in making this choice, thoughtfully consider your various options, and ultimately facilitate a (wedge-free) family selection about which you are all excited and confident.

How do you make a final college choice?

YOU *GET TO* DO THIS

Unless you apply under a binding decision plan (outlined in chapter 6), you will have until the National Candidate Reply Deadline of May 1 to make your final choice. If you are admitted early decision, you will need to close any outstanding applications. We recommend you do this immediately so that the other schools to which you have applied do not waste their time considering your application. It also means less emails for you and possibly creating an opportunity for a classmate—so win-win.

> For most students, the spring is about weighing options, comparing choices, and considering offers.

For most students, however, the spring is about weighing options, comparing choices, and considering offers.

Before we delve into how to do this, quickly look back over that last sentence—options, choices, and offers. If you are reading this chapter before the spring of senior year, you may question whether that will really be the case for you. Trust us: if you have followed the suggestions in this book, you will be admitted to a great match college that is capable of helping you grow, network, and achieve your goals. If you are reading it during this time of decision making—good job! We told you this would happen.

What a great spot to be in. Remember, having options was what this was all about. Ironically, often we hear students describe this choice as a burden rather than as a gift. We hope you will not view it as "I *have to* decide" but instead, "I *get to* decide." You *get to* think through the place you are going to thrive and create a lifelong network. You *get to* talk through your options with your family, who love you, are proud of you, and are excited about this next chapter of your life. You *get to* do this while finishing high school in a place that offers engaging classes, alongside peers who want to excel, and taught by teachers who are excited for you and want to see you continue to learn, grow, and succeed. You *get to* do this. What a privilege!

WHAT CAN YOU EXPECT FROM COLLEGES?

An utter blitzkrieg (look it up). Phone calls (to every number listed on your application), emails, texts, letters, owls, invitations, and random alumni knocking at your door. In chapter 2, we told you that "search" was big business. Well, "yield season" is search's first cousin. Get ready. Communication and marketing go into overdrive once you are admitted. The more students colleges can convert to deposits from their admitted pool, the fewer they will need to pull from the wait list. From a rankings and prestige standpoint, that is to their advantage because it keeps their admit rate lower and increases their yield rate.

You had to wait for months for an admission decision, and now the tables are turned. Colleges told you, "Just send your application, but don't call us or email because we are 'in committee.'" Now the tables are turned, and apparently they do not heed their own advice very well. We are not suggesting you put an auto response on your email telling them to check back in late April. Instead, we are just telling you to expect the full press.

They are going to invite you to admitted-student days or open houses. During these programs, you can count on hearing from amazing students, top faculty, successful alumni, and either the president or another high-level administrator. Generally, smaller schools will provide you the opportunity to interact with current students, visit a class, eat in a dining hall, tour campus, as well as explore your area of academic interest, and see a first-year residence hall. Larger, public universities may not be able to craft as personalized of an experience, but their admitted-student programs frequently allot time for you to speak with representatives from advising, housing, dining, orienta-tion, and other critical first-year support offices at tables during a fair-like portion of the day.

In recent years, colleges have invested thousands of dollars to cre-ate memorable experiences for admitted students that are specifically designed to connect them to one another. Programs often feature team competitions, scavenger hunts, off-campus excursions, and service projects, as well as games and activities intentionally crafted to help students meet one another, enjoy their time on campus, and get a feel for what the community will feel like as a student.

It is also common for colleges to host receptions geared toward connecting you with alumni, parents of current students, and other admitted students in your local area. Sometimes these are very ca-sual, and in other cases there will be a speaker and a formal program. These are low-cost, small-time-commitment opportunities to ask your questions and hear (typically in a far less scripted manner) from people in your community not only about their experiences on cam-pus but also how that school has affected their life in the longer term. We highly encourage you to attend these, ask questions, and grab a few business cards from local alumni. Focus especially on the other admitted students. Would you be excited to spend the next four years hanging out, learning, and traveling with these people?

You are going to receive letters, emails, and calls from people with titles you have never heard of (dean, chair, provost, registrar, bursar). Once you are admitted, the admission office essentially hands off your information to the community. They know that, in many ways, you are done with them, and it is now the full campus's job to recruit you. Expect to be contacted by faculty from your specific academic major, the athletic association, student groups, the orientation office, the outdoor recreation department, and at least one person named Matt or Katie. It can feel overwhelming at times.

Remember, you have until May 1. Your job is to keep asking your questions to as many people as possible during this time—they are just making that easier for you. Now on to what you need to do after you have been admitted and before making a final decision.

CELEBRATE YOUR CHOICES

We closed the last chapter with this, but it bears repeating: celebrate every admit. You worked hard to have each option, so enjoy and appreciate that accomplishment every time a letter arrives. Again, this does not have to be elaborate. We are not suggesting big parties or weekend trips. Instead, just promise us that you will take the time to do something private, personal, and meaningful as a family.

TAKE A CLOSER LOOK

Whether it has been six months, a year, or this is the first time you have visited, your lens as an admitted student is totally different than as a prospective applicant. At this point, you have a much more refined sense of what you want and need in your college experience. You also have (as predicted) other admission offers and will be making direct comparisons at this stage.

It is expensive to travel to these campuses, so do not just go along for the ride. Sticking with our car-buying metaphor, this is the time to "kick the wheels," test-drive each school, and not simply sit in the passenger's seat while the salesperson steers you through the experience. Be diligent about preparing ahead of time to ask the critical questions that have led you to this point and that you really want to have answered before making a final commitment.

What questions still linger, and who do you need to speak with to clarify those? What about the school do you feel confident about, and what do you need to make an effort to see while you are on campus? What are your top priorities for your college experience, and what details do you need to confirm those exist?

Remember, at this point, colleges are in promote-and-convert mode. Use that to your advantage by pressing them. It is fine to be honest about the other school(s) to which you have been admitted and ask them to outline differences in academic programs, campus culture, outcomes, return on investment—to really distinguish themselves. You will feel far more confident when you leave if you can get them to specifically state what makes them different, unique, and the best choice for you.

Maybe you need to learn more about career services and internship opportunities, or perhaps you are curious about how accessible research positions are early in your undergraduate career. If you have a documented learning issue, you probably want to know more details about student support, tutoring, and accommodations. You may want to find out about specific affinity groups on campus and the campus culture around inclusion and diversity. Plan to visit the specific academic department in which you are interested and talk with professors, advisors, and current students about their areas of concentration and scholarly work. Matthew DeGreeff, the dean of college counseling and student enrichment at Middlesex School, says to students, "Ask schools, 'When I have to do hard things well—in terms of academics, social, artistic, and/or athletics—who will be there to guide me and support me?'"

Remember, you are the customer, and you are investing your time and money to make this important decision—dig below the surface. The reaction of community members to your exploration will be telling. Is the campus generally welcoming? Do people go out of their way to greet you, congratulate you, and help you feel like part of the family? Are answers consistent between faculty, administrators, and students? If you find great variance, you will need to determine whether that's an indication of limitless possibilities or a campus culture that is not truly distinct. Don't take any one person's opinion as gospel truth. No one person is the expert on all things about a college or university. Your goal is to hear as many perspectives as possible. Debra Johns, the associate director of admissions at Yale University, advises, "Look at *anything* provided by students. Pay attention to the tone on admitted student websites. Does it resonate with you or not? Ask, 'Can I see myself growing, stretching and evolving here? Will this be an incredible journey? Will I be challenged on every single level at some point during my four years?'"

Hear as many perspectives as possible.

As you spend time on each campus, ask yourself the following and consider the advice of college admission professionals who have guided thousands of admitted students through this experience.

Will You Feel Comfortable?

You should continually be asking whether you feel at home when you walk on the campus of schools that have offered you admission. Your goal is to find a place where you can challenge yourself to continually learn, grow, and thrive. Do not overlook or undervalue the basics. Talk to current college students, and they will tell you—especially if you have specific allergies, dietary restrictions, or preferences—food matters. Likewise, be sure to visit the first-year residence halls, even if they are not part of the formal tour. They are not going to compare to your room at home, but rest is critical to both your mental and physical health, so pay attention. Do not discount the importance of finding a space where you can recharge, study, and socialize.

Find **Your** *Answers*

Food

- Does the meal plan allow for flexibility, or is it limited in choice?
- Are you required to carry the school's plan in your first year only or throughout your entire time on campus?
- Are there spaces where you can cook for yourself?
- Are there ample gluten-free, kosher, or nondairy options?
- Are there local grocery stores and restaurants that provide food options to supplement campus offerings?

Housing

- Are there substance-free housing options if this is a priority for you?
- Are single-gender floors or residence halls available?
- Are there gender-expansive/nonconforming housing or bathrooms?

- Can first-year students have single rooms, or are double rooms, suites, triples, or apartment-style set-ups the standard?

Will You Feel Safe?

This is more likely to be at the top of your parents' list, but you also need to feel like you can take risks and learn without fear, ridicule, or harm. Look beyond the blue lights. Colleges will often point to the security call stations situated throughout campus as an indication of a safe environment. Do not settle for this baseline standard. Find out what security concerns exist on campus and what the most recent cases have been. The campus newspaper and open campus community forums and social media are good sources of information to learn about police presence, security issues and prevention strategies, student perceptions surrounding safety, and the frequency and specifics of incidents. Seek out a broad range of perspectives—current students, alumni, faculty, staff—to gain a clear picture of the environment on campus. The Clery Act mandates that colleges provide a report of campus crime, so be a smart consumer in obtaining this information. From sexual assault statistics to theft to hazing, you will be able to get a clear picture of the safety climate on campus. Beyond your physical safety, is the academic culture one in which you will be challenged intellectually and have the ability to express your opinions in an open, honest, respectful, and encouraging atmosphere? Reflect on your high school experience to determine what you are and are not looking for inside and outside the classroom.

> Your goal is to determine whether you are excited about becoming a part of your chosen campus's community.

Find Your *Answers*

Physical Safety

- What systems are in place for campus alerts or emergency notification? How are parents made aware of crime or other incidents that occur on campus?

- What is the highest-profile crime reported on campus in the past year? How does that compare to other schools you are considering, other colleges in the area, and your city or hometown?

- How safe is the neighborhood/area surrounding campus?

- What is the relationship like between the college and the town?

- What are the campus statistics for reports of dating violence, domestic violence, sexual assault, and stalking?

- What procedures exist for institutional disciplinary action in cases of dating violence, domestic violence, sexual assault, stalking, and other crimes?

- Does campus security provide a safe escort service in the evening, and if so, how accessible is it and how often is it used?

Intellectual Safety

- What is the academic climate on campus like?

- How supportive is the community of freedom of expression (inside and outside the classroom)?

- Are students and faculty open to diverse opinions and perspectives? Do they "talk across the aisle"?

- Has the campus hosted controversial speakers, and what was the community's response?

- What is the academic culture around "trigger warnings"?

Will You Belong?

Do you feel a sense of community, connection, and belonging on campus? If colleges have done their job in telling their unique story, and if you have done your research and really listened, it will be evident that each campus has its own distinct culture, ethos, and dynamic. A key part of making your college choice is about finding *your* people. Do you get a sense of belonging? Your job is to determine whether you are excited and confident about becoming a part of that campus community. Is it a school where you can be yourself?

Find **Your** *Answers*
- Who are the types of people that challenge, support, stretch, and encourage you?

- What types of individuals do you like to surround yourself with?

- Are you looking for a college experience that mirrors your home / high school or one that takes you completely outside your comfort zone and exposes you to a completely new and different culture?

- Do you want a college that has a lot of school spirit?

- Are students engaged in and out of class?

- What do students do on weekends?

- Is it a "suitcase campus," where students tend to go their separate ways when classes are done?

- How connected are the alumni? Is there a strong network that persists beyond the campus gates?

- If you are honest, do you really see yourself there?

It's not life or death. Don't get caught up in prestige or what you are going to study as the likelihood is you will change your mind and discover new academic interests. You are not going to study 24/7. Make sure whatever are your passions/interests/activities that at least a few of them are available and open to you regardless of your proposed major or activity. —Spike Gummere, Special Assistant to the President, Lake Forest College

---

Can You Be Successful?

In his book *David and Goliath: Underdogs, Misfits, and the Art of Battling Giants*, Malcolm Gladwell explores unlikely outcomes and the dangers of comparing oneself to others. He details the story of a young woman who attended Brown University rather than the University of Maryland. She struggled in chemistry—her chosen field—because of feelings of inadequacy that may not have plagued her elsewhere. The choices we make determine the quality and direction of our lives. Which of your college options is the best match for you in the short and long term?

Find **Your** *Answers*

- In the past, what experiences and environments have provided you with the encouragement and inspiration to grow?

- Will the culture, faculty, and fellow students at the school offer the freedom you need to be proud of your accomplishments and to both discover and enhance your talents and abilities?

- In college, do you want to be a "big fish" in a small pond or "small fish" in a big pond?

- Do you sense this is a place you will spend your college experience feeling like you don't measure up, or is it a place that will inspire you to find confidence in your potential to excel?

"Will I grow?"—rather than looking for a college that suits exactly who you are, I think it ideal to choose a college where there's at least some sense that you'll have to grow into it. Since I would hold that you shouldn't leave college being the same person you were when you started, I think you can't find the growth if you go to a campus that feels perfect in every way. —Jim Rawlins, Assistant Vice President and Director of Admission, University of Oregon

Can I identify three specific ways I'm excited to make community and make my mark here? —Kelly Talbert, Director of Admissions, Boise State University

What am I good at? Too much focus on prestige and what will "appear" to be the best choice rather than which option will allow the student to discover their talents. —Patrick Winter, Assistant Vice President, University of Georgia

Can You Thrive?

The temptation, at any age, is to focus on the short term or the immediate. This is completely understandable because we are constantly barraged with advertisements, sales pitches, and social media that implore us to opt for the quick fix or the "today only" sale. On his leadership podcast, Andy Stanley discusses the concept of "self-leadership." He outlines the dichotomy between the immediate and the ultimate. The immediate, he says, is what is right in front of us. It is based on wants, image, and so on. In contrast, the ultimate centers on values. Who are you? Who do you want to be? What are your values, and, importantly, do you resonate with and gain inspiration from the values of those around you? These are big questions and a challenge to discern at any age. But they are critical to helping you make a final college decision.

Find Your Answers

- Put simply, which college will allow you to be your best self?

- As you consider college options, what resources and supports exist on each campus to help you reach your goals?

- Are you interested in double majoring or pursuing a minor? If so, how flexible is the curriculum?

- Do you want the ability to delve immediately into your major, or do you want a school that provides breadth and depth of offerings necessary to allow for exploration?

- How accessible are opportunities for creativity?

- What are your desires for your college experience, and will your choice provide a framework for you to achieve these hopes?

Students and families need to be asking about outcomes and how the school they attend will help them achieve goals they never thought possible. Students seem to be missing the idea that college is about exploring new areas they do not have any experience in and finding what they want to do and create for themselves after attending. Schools that have a history of transforming students into creative thinkers are rich learning environments and families should be asking how a student is supported through a kind of learning that encourages creativity and pushes the limits of a student's experience. —George Zimmerman, Executive Director of Admissions and Recruitment, West Virginia University

---

RUN THE NUMBERS

In the television show *Lost* (bar none the best American series of all time), Hurley (Jorge Garcia) has a number of flashbacks that depict him winning millions of dollars in a lottery using the numbers 4.8.15.16.23.42. Immediately afterward he begins to witness his friends, family, and coworkers suffering horrible misfortunes and accidents. Ultimately, he ends up in a mental asylum where another patient explains with horror, "The numbers are bad! You gotta get away from them!" Well, the numbers you heard as a prospective student are not bad now, but they are fundamentally different as an admitted student. They mean more, and they are critical to the equation of your final choice. So do not run from them—embrace them.

Reexamine starting salaries of students from the schools you have been admitted to—specifically in the major you plan to study. Look closely at the average debt load and repayment timeline of graduates. Explore the number of employers that come to campus to hire current students for internships or co-ops and that recruit graduating students for jobs. Evaluate the published return on investment numbers that *Forbes*, *Kiplingers*, *Money*, and other national publications publish. These will typically take starting salaries, midcareer earnings, and overall costs into consideration for their methodology, but be sure you understand the formulas they are using to arrive at their conclusions.

When you receive financial aid packages, be diligent about comparing them to one another. We highly recommend you create a spreadsheet specifically for this purpose. What does each school expect you to pay back (loans)? How much are they giving you in merit- or need-based scholarship that you will not need to pay back? Is the award renewable or only good for one year? Does your aid package include an assumption that you will have an on-campus job? Are they including Parent PLUS Loans?

Generally, you will have all of these financial aid packages by the last week of March or first week of April at the latest. This still gives you nearly a month to make a final choice. Do not be in a rush. Frequently, families do not completely understand their financial aid awards (and unfortunately they are all different in format and terminology), so do not hesitate to call the financial aid office to speak directly with a representative about your specific package and the implications for you both as a student and a graduate. While you are on the call, or if you visit in person, be sure to ask about subsequent years. Are there departmental grants or scholarships that you may qualify for after your first year? Do aid packages for first-year students typically look more generous than those of upper-class students? What will change when your older brother graduates from college next year or your younger sister begins college the following year? The numbers are not bad, but they can be tricky. No question is off limits, so keep asking and pressing until you are comfortable and confident that you understand exactly what your real cost will be to attend.

Ask each college the often overlooked, "What is your retention rate to the second year?" and "What is the *four*-year graduation rate?" —Mike Sexton, Vice President for Enrollment Management, Santa Clara University

---

TRUST YOUR GUT

Ultimately, only you can make this decision. It is said, "The road of life is paved with flat squirrels who could not make a decision." Don't be that squirrel. Remember, this is not life or death; nor is it about being wrong or right on a multiple-choice test. It may sound trite but it is true: you know you. Be confident and trust your gut.

In the end, you need to trust your gut.

Closing other doors is never easy. This is the first of many times you will experience these types of choices: relationships, jobs, graduate school, or moving to a new city or state or country. Sometimes, the hardest part about being talented—the most difficult part about having options— is that there really is not a definitively *right* answer. Perhaps Steve Jobs said it best in his 2005 Stanford commencement address: "Your time is limited, so don't waste it living someone else's life. Don't be trapped by dogma—which is living with the results of other people's thinking. Don't let the noise of others' opinions drown out your own inner voice. And most important, have the courage to follow your heart and intuition. They somehow already know what you truly want to become. Everything else is secondary" (Jobs 2005).

Here are some thoughts from admission professionals to consider if you are trying to figure out if you just ate something that is not sitting well or if it is actually a prodding to pick a certain college.

Close your eyes. When I say go, what college campus are you standing on? You are making a decision for one year. You will make the best decision for yourself at this time with the information you have now. If after you attend a school and the information you know changes, you can always make another decision. Try not to place the pressure of "this one decision will affect the rest of my life" on yourself. Life is a series of choices and decisions. —Sally O'Rourke, Director of College Counseling, Mercersburg Academy

Ask each college, "What is the most important character aspect of this school?" It helps separate schools beyond programs, aid packages, and rankings and allows the school to have its own "personality" among others in the same genre of school. —Whitney Soule, Dean of Admission and Financial Aid, Bowdoin College

Choosing a college is often more of an emotional decision as it is rational one. This is why I recommend students honestly and objectively consider what they really want from their college experience, and how the colleges they are considering match their expectations. College is a big investment of time and money, so you want to make the right decision for the right reasons. —Scott Verzyl, Dean of Undergraduate Admissions, University of South Carolina

Choosing your college is like buying a pair of jeans. You bring many into the dressing room and choose the pair that feels the best, and is within your budget, out of the available options. They may fit well, but are far from perfect when brand new. It's only after wearing them, and washing them over time, that they become truly comfortable. That's like college—over time, you make new friends, choose interesting and challenging classes, get involved in your new community and declare a major. All of these experiences, over time, help the college fit even better. There is no one perfect fit, there will be good and bad classroom experiences, defining friendships and emotional hardships, unexpected and inspiring opportunities at all the schools you consider. Compromise is inevitable and no college/university is tailor made for you. The things that might make you uncomfortable at first may bring the most personal growth and help launch you into a fulfilling life. —Ann Marie Strauss, Director of College Counseling, Garrison Forest School

Follow your heart, considering your head and your wallet. —Miguel Wasielewski, Executive Director of Admissions, University of Texas at Austin

Start with thinking hard (and honestly) about what matters most to you, what situations, circumstances, etc., make you smile most often and then look at your school options and consider where you are likely to smile more often and for the most reasons. Ask each college, "What are the top 2 or 3 reasons that students choose to leave your school?" —Eric Monheim, Director of College Counseling, St. Mark's School

College is about meaningful engagement with others who don't share your worldview. Think of yourself as a rubber band. Choose the school that stretches you the most without breaking you. Ask which college's core values most closely resemble yours. —Heath Einstein, Dean of Admission, Texas Christian University

Think carefully about choosing a college mainly because of the big, fun athletic program, especially football—because that only covers 4, maybe 5 Saturdays (home games) out of the entire school year. Sure, those 4 or 5 days will be fun, but you need to think about how you will feel about your choice of college on a rainy Tuesday afternoon in February when the campus is quiet. —Catherine Odum, Associate Director of College Guidance, Charlotte Country Day School

Look for a place where the energy will get you to engage in several areas. Ask each college, "What are some of the opportunities here that are not to be missed?" —Sheppard Shanley, Senior Associate Director of Admission, Northwestern University

BURN THE SHIPS!

In 1519, Hernán Cortés sailed to Veracruz, Mexico, on the direction of the king and queen of Spain, to find gold, silver, and a new place to settle. When they arrived, his crew talked incessantly about returning home. They were thinking about other places and imagining a different life. As they came ashore, Cortés ordered, "Burn the ships!" so that they would not look back and instead would be fully committed to this new land and life.

Once you put down your deposit, that is your job as well. (Yes, it's unpaid, but the returns are incalculable.) You need to be all-in—buy the T-shirt, put the window decal on the car, be confident in your decision. Start following student groups on social media from that campus, donate or trade the shirts you have from other schools (you don't have to go all Cortés here and burn them), close/cancel your applications from other colleges, and start planning on going to orientation in the summer. Be thankful for the ability to choose, refuse to allow buyer's remorse to get the best of you, and move forward confidently.

———

Guard yourself from the temptation to think the grass is greener elsewhere. Begin your conversations with others and within yourself with an attitude of gratitude for the opportunities you have rather than a spirit of entitlement or loss. —Michael Schell, Director of College Counseling, Catholic Memorial School

———

MAY 1 MEANS BY THAT NIGHT

If you do not deposit by 11:59 p.m. on May 1 and an admission director comes in the morning of May 2 over their class target, they are going to immediately shut down the ability for admitted students to pay additional deposits. It is now possible to set their system to close on May 2 at 12:01 a.m. (Please don't ask about time zones.) Make your choice and put your money down. Burn the ships! Deadline means *deadline*.

⚙ *Try This*

1. Narrow your choices down to one to four schools.

2. Visit each college, either during accepted-student events or on your own.

3. After your visits, write down the strengths and weaknesses (pros/cons) of each college. Create categories and make strength/weakness lists for each area that matters the most to you (academics, social life, athletics, food, etc.). Can you narrow your choices at all? Is one list of pros longer than the other?

4. Role-play: choose a college and spend three days telling yourself that is where you are going. Wear the shirt, hat, or hoodie. Put their pennant up in your room. Sit with it. Say it out loud. For those few days, try to put the other options out of your mind, and just be aware of your reactions to your decision. During that time, are you excited, relieved, regretful, anxious, hopeful? How does it feel? Jot down your reactions. When those three days are up, repeat the exercise with each college that is on your final list.

💬 Talk About This

1. What are the main factors holding you back from making a decision?

2. Is there information you still need to gather before you can decide? If so, what do you need to know and how will you get answers?

3. What are other big decisions that you or your family have made, and how did you go about making them? What can you learn from those experiences?

👍 **CHECK IN** After reading this chapter, are you still on the same page? If you are not all-in together, what do you need to do, discuss, or learn to get there?

CHAPTER 10

Closing Letters

Get up everybody and sing / Everyone can see we're together /
As we walk on by / And we fly just like birds of a feather.
"WE ARE FAMILY" BY SISTER SLEDGE

YOUR HOMEWORK: A COLLEGE COUNSELOR'S LETTER TO STUDENTS

He who has a why to live for can bear almost any how.
—Friedrich Wilhelm Nietzsche

Call it a rite of passage, a journey, a process, or an experience, but essentially college admission asks, who are you and what do you want? Easy, right? As we close out this book, I (Brennan) have two home-work assignments for you. Don't worry, there are no worksheets and you will not be graded. In fact, if you have learned anything in these pages, it should be that searching for and applying to college is not a test or project that you can, or should attempt to, ace. Even better news: the due date for these assignments is flexible. I just want you to consider them prerequisites to being prepared to take advantage of the opportunities this experience presents. The first piece of homework is an activity, possibly the most important you will do. The second is some required reading; though in truth, I will provide you with some CliffsNotes to highlight the take-home messages. All you really need is an open mind and the continued willingness to approach college admission grounded in family and future. Are you ready?

DO THIS

First some background: When I was in my early thirties, my mother (then in her late fifties) was diagnosed with early-onset Alzheimer's disease and frontal-lobe dementia. This began a five-year deterioration of her memory. Did she remember all of the special moments from my childhood? Did she remember driving me and my brothers from activity to activity? Did she remember the battles we had about homework? Did she know how selfless she had been since the day I was born? Did she remember our visits to colleges and the laughs we shared as I dreamed about my future and she hesitantly anticipated my departure? Did she know how grateful I was? Did she know how much I loved her? I assumed she did, but how often did I intentionally say it beyond signing off from a phone call or departing for a trip?

OK, now the activity: When you finish reading this paragraph, put the book down and go find your parents. Look them in the eyes, and tell them that you need them to know that *you love them* and *you appreciate them.* (You can add a hug for emphasis.) It is that simple: "I love you" and "Thank you." Don't laugh it off with sarcasm as you tell them. Don't text it to them. Don't dismiss this exercise because your love and appreciation is "a given" or "no-brainer." Choose to express yourself and acknowledge the awesome power they have given you. OK . . . now go. I will be waiting.

Welcome back. It felt good, right? It seems trivial, but you are *where* you are, and in many ways *who* you are, because of them. This exercise is a framework for approaching college admission. This experience is about relationships, communication, gratitude, and choice. Prioritizing relationships and investing in people will not only dictate how successful your college search and application experience is but will have implications for your college career and life well beyond it. While you may be the one applying, the college admission experience is a team effort that requires communicating honestly, frequently, and openly, in order to stay unified. Do not try to go at this alone. Express your love and gratitude early and often.

READ THIS

Every great course has a robust syllabus of readings to guide your learning experience. The following books provide important lessons and questions that will make your college search more meaningful. I know: you are busy, and who has time to read more than what is already assigned in school? Don't worry, I am going to make this easy with a synopsis and take-home message for you to consider. For extra credit, check out the list of books and other resources in the appendix.

Start with Why: How Great Leaders Inspire Everyone to Take Action by Simon Sinek

Synopsis: As the title suggests, Sinek stresses the importance of understanding why we do what we do. If you don't have the time to read the book, at the very least watch his wildly popular TED Talk and listen to the ways that he weaves together examples of inspirational leaders such as Dr. Martin Luther King Jr., inventors like the Wright brothers, and business innovators like Steve Jobs. The tie that binds these individuals is their ability to focus less on the outcome and more on articulating the reason behind their intentions and actions.

Key Quote: "Knowing your WHY is not the only way to be successful, but it is the only way to maintain lasting success and have a greater blend of innovation and flexibility. When a WHY goes fuzzy, it becomes much more difficult to maintain the growth, loyalty and inspiration that helped drive the original success."

The Take-Home: I know, we have driven this message into the ground throughout the book—that you must first connect with your *why*. You are probably sick of hearing it, but it is at the core of our philosophy. Admission to college is not a passive experience; it is about engagement, and I am challenging you to lean in. My hope is that you will have the confidence to not simply submit to the expectations of those around you. And that extends well beyond college admission. Use this as an opportunity to ask yourself *why*—and then enjoy seeing the *where* and *what* follow.

This is the ideal time to really consider who you are and explore your vision for the future. I see too many students buy into the myth that college admission is merely something to "get through" and that it is a stressful experience that requires needlessly jumping through hoops. Sure, it takes planning, work, and compromise, and there will be parts of this journey that will be more enjoyable (maybe college visits) than others (perhaps standardized testing). However, if you stay true to yourself and keep your hopes for the future front and center, it will become less of a chore and more of an adventure.

> **This is the ideal time to consider who you are and explore your vision for the future.**

Applying to college is not just about submitting applications and waiting for a reply. It is about envisioning the years to come and the experiences you hope to have. We have provided many questions for you to ask yourself throughout this book. Here are a few themes to consider in closing: What are you excited about? What are you scared of? What do you want to be different in your next chapter? What is something new you hope to try? Who do you want to meet? What do you want to learn that you have not yet had the opportunity to explore? Think big, and let your college search and application support these dreams.

Where You Go Is Not Who You'll Be: An Antidote to the College Admission Mania by Frank Bruni

Synopsis: Again, the title says it all. In this important study of college outcomes, Bruni asks us all to take a deep collective breath and realize that admission to any given school does not guarantee success, happiness, or meaning. Using stories and statistics about well-known people, he lays out a case for applying to and attending schools of all shapes and sizes.

Key Quote: "The nature of a student's college experience—the work that he or she puts into it, the skills he or she picks up, the self-examination that's undertaken, the resourcefulness that's honed—matters more than the name of the institution attended."

The Take-Home: Are you a quantitative or data-driven person? Do you need reassurance that life will still work out if you are denied at your top-choice college and have to "settle" for a school farther down your list? Bruni's book demonstrates the point we have repeatedly made—there is no perfect or dream college. Your goal is a perfect approach, one of connection, confidence, and collaboration. (Oh . . . and don't worry, we have your backs. We are telling your parents they need to read it too.)

The Road to Character by **David Brooks**

Synopsis: Through a study of great leaders and activists, Brooks invites us to consider the aspects of character that really matter. This *New York Times* columnist is adept at capturing the human condition. In his book, Brooks outlines "eulogy virtues"—those things you are and will always be known for, the contributions you make to others and the joy you bring to life. These qualities, far more than any list of achievements or awards you may have won (what he calls "résumé virtues"), are what distinguish and separate you.

Key Quote: "People with character may be loud or quiet, but they do tend to have a certain level of self-respect. Self-respect is not the same as self-confidence or self-esteem. Self-respect is not based on IQ or any of the mental or physical gifts that help you get into a competitive college. It is not comparative. It is not earned by being better than other people at something. It is earned by being better than you used to be, by being dependable at times of testing, straight in times of temptation. It emerges in one who is morally dependable. Self-respect is produced by inner triumphs, not external ones."

The Take-Home: So much of college admission can seem like résumé building. "What activities *should* I do?" "What classes *do I need to* take?" "Which essay topic *must* I choose?" It is too easy to focus on the selection part of college admission and to view it as a judgment on you as a person. Having worked with hundreds and hundreds of college applicants, I continually hear students ask themselves: "Will I measure up?" "Will I stand out?" "Will I get in?" "Will I be successful?" The answer, unequivocally, is yes. I will say that again: *yes.*

No matter where you end up, you are going to be an invaluable addition to that campus community. My hope is that you'll not waiver from that belief.

IF YOU REMEMBER ANYTHING . . .

When I was first starting out in education, a colleague suggested that when planning my classes for the year, I consider what "beach knowledge" I wanted my students to have. What he meant by this was that when they are sitting on the beach in July, what should students remember about my class and what they learned. So, now that you have faithfully completed your homework above, here is the beach knowledge I want you to take with you. As you go through your college experience, my hope is that you will add to this list and really take this to heart.

College Admission *Is*

- A personal journey: this is your search, so own it.

- An invitation to explore identity and purpose: this will not happen overnight.

- Imperfect: it is human process, so expect "user error."

- A celebration of your hard work.

- About engagement: so lean in.

- Fun: the minute it becomes a chore, stop and check yourself; enjoy the ride.

- An investment in you: both short and long term.

- About unity not vanity: so don't sacrifice relationships for status.

- A privilege: so take advantage of the opportunities you have.

- Full of choice: so be open and consider all of your options.

College Admission Is *Not*

- A value judgment on whether you are "good enough."

- Life or death.

- Fair.

- About status: aim high but for the right reasons.

- A game or prize.

- The final exam for high school: you only do high school once, so live in it.

- One size fits all.

- To be taken at face value: dig deep and ask probing questions.

- A reason to create an unreasonable schedule: so prioritize balance.

- A passive experience: you are in control, so assert it.

- A search for perfection: there is not one "right" college.

- A test: like life, this is the real thing, so be in it.

Here is what I know—you are bound for success. You are bound for an exciting college experience filled with opportunities to learn, connect, and grow. *Where* all of that will happen is a mystery—and like all good mysteries, it should be filled with twists, turns, discovery, new places, and interesting people. My hope is that you will find joy in uncovering the clues that lead you and that ultimately you will arrive on a college campus confident and excited to embrace opportunity.

KEEPING IT SIMPLE: AN ADMISSION DEAN'S LETTER TO PARENTS

I (Rick) will never forget the day my wife, Amy, and I told my parents that she was pregnant with our first child. We were at our favorite restaurant in town, and when the bill came, I leaned across the table to grab it. My dad, as expected, simultaneously reached for his wallet. "Don't worry, Grandpa. I got it," I said, as I slid the sonogram over to him and my mom.

After some hugs and tears, they conveyed their congratulations, while we shared our excitement and confessed our nervousness. As usual, my mom's words were succinct and poignant: "There is no 100-percent right way. Just make sure your kids always know you love them and that you are proud of them. Everything else will take care of itself." Since that time, we have received plenty of parenting advice (largely unsolicited) about everything from swaddling to school choice, diapers to discipline, and car seats to summer camps. To this day, however, my mom's words remain the most instructive.

So, I'm going to take a page from her book and keep my advice (and hopes) for your family's college admission experience very simple.

Change Your Filter

I grew up in Decatur, Georgia. At the time, it was . . . fine. Lots of auto shops, a few good burger options, and the standard churches, recreation centers, schools, and city services of most towns.

My street was divided—half the houses were in the city limits of Decatur, and half were in the county (DeKalb). As kids, we did not think much of it, other than that the city sign made good target practice for an array of launched objects. Adults agreed (not about the sign) that there was basically no distinguishable difference in quality between county and city. When I went to college in North Carolina, nobody had heard of Decatur, so I would simply say I grew up a few miles east of downtown Atlanta.

Today is a different story. The standard three-bedroom, two-bath houses that once filled Decatur are largely gone. It is tough to find anything on the market for less than $500,000, and new construction commonly approaches seven figures. People living on the city line now vehemently petition for annexation; the gas stations have been converted to gastropubs (that will gladly charge you $15 for "frites"); boutiques line the streets; the school system is among the best in the state; and the quality of life is continually touted in trendy national magazines—even the city sign is nicer.

Bottom line: Decatur has become a destination. You simply cannot apply the same filter you did 20 years ago, or even 5 years for that matter.

As you go through the college admission experience, I hope you will keep an open mind, "look beyond what you see," and *change your filter.* Basically everything has changed—the way students search for schools, the format and content of applications, the volume and competition, and importantly the reputation and brand of many universities.

Look beyond what you see.

Then

"The University of X? Where the kids from our school went if they could not get into ... ?"

"If you drove slowly down Main Street with your window open, they'd throw a diploma in."

"On Tuesdays people were already tailgating for Saturday's game."

Now

Yeah, yeah, I know. I'm telling you, Decatur was a little sketchy. I distinctly remember looking askance at the lollipops bank tellers would hand out. So when your student brings you a brochure from the University of X, I'm hoping you will consider it with a fresh set of eyes. That college town is now consistently written up in major national magazines as a great place for food, family, and culture; the university has invested heavily in student support and programs; their students are winning international competitions for research and prestigious scholarships and fellowships. Change your filter. Good old U of X may be a great match. Don't dilute their excitement with preconceived notions.

Then

"He has a 1460. He'll get in for sure."

"They gave me a summer provisional admit offer, and I was able to stay if I did well."

"I wrote a two-word essay: 'Go' followed by their mascot, which I misspelled, and they still let me in."

Now

I hear you: 1460 is a high test score. You should be proud and impressed. And you are right, 20 or more years ago there was room for "creative admission" practices at colleges that now admit less than one of every three applicants and carry wait lists with as many applicants as applied the year you started college. There was a time when, even at highly selective schools, it was basically about the numbers (and the relationships, but we won't delve into that here), so good grades and solid testing were a likely combination for being admitted.

Thankfully, as we have established, there are still many great colleges running numeric formulas to make their decisions. However, if your child chooses to apply to schools receiving far more applications than they have spaces in their class, I hope you will change your filter and not make any assumptions. Holistic admission means that test scores and GPA are only a small piece of a much larger conversation that also includes discussions around impact, influence, and institutional priorities.

Then

"Tuition was less than $1,000 per quarter."

"I paid my next semester's bill with the money I saved from my internship."

"I was able to pay off all of my student loans within five years of graduating."

Now

In today's market, you have as much of a chance buying a new house in Decatur for $200 as $200,000. As you begin to research college costs, you'll likely have some eye-popping, heart-stopping, head-shaking moments. I hope you will not let tuition or overall cost of attendance alone keep you from visiting a school or encouraging your student to apply if you all determine it is a good match academically, geographically, and culturally.

I hope you will be humble enough to share your financial situation openly and early with your student. Walk them through your limitations, conditions, and expectations that we discussed in chapter 3. If you will give them the credit of knowing and understanding this information, you will be amazed by the respect with which they absorb and apply it. Take the time to have honest conversations about finances, do your homework early by checking out colleges' net price calculators, and start reading up on different financial aid packages and programs. One of the biggest gifts you can give your student in this experience is helping to educate them about financial choices and the implications various loan amounts will have both during college and after they graduate.

You can find many affordable financial matches. I hope you will direct your family to identify and select one of these rather than overextend financially and incur burdensome student or parent loan debt.

A Special Note to Alumni

"I have been donating consistently for the last 20 years."

"There should be spots held for families who have multiple-generation connections."

"Don't y'all care at all about preserving tradition? We've been bringing our kids there since they were in diapers."

If you loved your college experience, changing the filter of your own alma mater is sometimes the toughest. It is understandable for you to want your child to visit and apply, but my hope is that you will remain objective as they consider whether it is a good match with their goals.

One of the biggest tragedies I see is the reaction of alumni when their kids are not admitted. They take it as a personal affront and let it taint their own experience and love for the school. Commit early to not letting that be part of your story. Before you write your college out of your will, cancel your season tickets, or remove a tattoo, remember that the way admission decisions *feel* are not how they are *made*.

Ultimately, I hope you will have the vision to help your student start by asking *why* they want to go to college, the patience to listen and thoughtfully consider their answers, and the wisdom to keep bringing them back to those guiding responses along the way. Allow their goals and hopes rather than an arbitrary list, the opinions of others, the culture of your school or community, a rankings guide with subjective methodology, or outdated stereotypes to lead your exploration.

Control What You Can Control

You cannot control admission decisions. You cannot control institutional priorities or merit scholarships or financial aid packages. You cannot control the competition in any given applicant pool. You can control how you conduct yourself and the example you set for those around you.

I hope you will be an example in your community. At times the swirling discussions about college and gossip about admissions will be unhealthy and unproductive. I hope you will recognize these moments and either remove yourself entirely or redirect the conversation. When a friend's son gets admitted to college, share in their joy. When your daughter's teammate is dejected about not being admitted, encourage her with what you know—she is going to have many other incredible choices. Tell her with confidence and excitement that good news is coming.

I hope you will be an example on social media. You are going to see some terribly misinformed opinions, negative banter, catty comments, and bald-faced lies. I hope you will not engage in that dialogue online and take the opportunities in person to recenter your friends, neighbors, or relatives. Strongly consider not posting anything about your child's college search or admission experience, unless you think it could be beneficial to others who are part of your online community. I hope you will use your platform to be encouraging, positive, and reassuring. Provide healthy and desperately needed perspective to online discussions when they go off the rails and fan the flames of anxiety.

I hope you will be an example for your family. Back away when you are at a college visit, and let your student ask the questions of a tour guide or an admission counselor. In a short year or two, they will be on a college campus. They will need to be able to advocate and navigate for themselves to professors and in internship or job interviews. I hope you will see this as an opportunity to prepare them for success in that chapter.

I hope that as a parent in this process, you will remember that you are more of a coach than a player. You are a parent—not an applicant. That is so much easier said than done. I hope you will go for a walk or a drive when you hear yourself say things like "*We* are taking the SAT next weekend" or "*Our* first choice is Vanderbilt." Ask yourself if those pronouns are just a reflection of your love and 17 years of intimately intertwined lives, or if they are a subtle indication that you should step back and let your student demonstrate what you know they are capable of handling. Parenting is a delicate dance, but it is one you know well. Be honest with yourself, and you will know when and when not to take the lead. You got this!

Trust your child's ability to articulate points and express themselves effectively in writing for colleges. Use your weekly meetings to ask questions about college essays and make helpful edits or suggestions rather than rewrite their work or insert words like "prodigious" or "convivial."

You are going to see inequities. You will see students "get in" with lower scores than your own child. The kid down the street / the blue-chip athlete / the son of a major donor (insert unthinkable prototype here) is going to receive offers or scholarships or opportunities that your student does not. You are going to read online or see on social media videos, pictures, comments, and posts about neighbors or students in your school or community who by every measure you can observe do not seem "as good as" or "as qualified as" your kid.

Each year, after decisions go out, admission officers receive fuming phone calls, vitriolic emails, threats, accusations of bias or conspiracy, and expletive-laden rants. These are *never* from students. I hope that when you are tempted to "get in my car and drive down there," you will take a deep breath and (when necessary) bite your lip. When you get upset or frustrated or angry, my hope is that you remember that those emotions are actually just a manifestation of your love for your child. They need to hear it, so keep telling them (even when they act like they know or don't hear you).

I hope that you will encourage your child to enjoy their high school years. Remind them to keep perspective when a test does not go well or a final grade is lower than they had hoped. If they want to quit a team or an activity because they are absolutely miserable, give them that space. Hug them often. Enjoy this unique, special, and all-too-short chapter of life.

It Is All Going to Work Out

My hope is that you will not get stuck in an echo chamber when your student is in high school and especially when they are looking at and applying to colleges. Find ways to continually break out of that. I hope you will take some time to look at the Fortune 500 or Fortune 100 list of companies and their CEOs. Most graduated from schools that are *not* categorized as highly selective. Go back and reread Frank Bruni's book *Where You Go Is Not Who You'll Be.* Listen to the many stories that your own friends and colleagues will tell about their own college experiences. They will tell you about how they did not get into their top choice or could not afford to attend a certain school, and now 20–30 years after graduating, they would not have it any other way.

Talk to parents who have kids in college. Ask them to reflect on their experience. Inevitably, you will hear them say they wish they had not stressed as much about everything. They will tell you about their daughter who was not admitted to her first-choice school, ended up elsewhere, and is thriving now. They will go into great detail about how their son did not receive the merit scholarship he had hoped for, selected another option from his choices, and now has an incredible internship and a girlfriend (whom they actually like) whom he would never have met otherwise.

I understand that as a parent, the college admission experience seems incredibly complicated, because it is filled with a myriad of dates and deadlines. It seems confusing because the mainstream press and pervasive "how-to guides" regularly provide incomplete, and frequently inaccurate, data. It seems consuming because friends and colleagues incessantly share their "inside" information and stories (or the alleged stories of relatives twice removed) on social media. It seems confounding because those same friends and colleagues, while adamant, have widely divergent experiences and opinions that they are quick to share each time they see you at the school, store, or stadium. It seems complex because colleges and universities all have different processes, review different factors, and operate on different timelines.

> **Keep it simple—love your kids well.**

After watching this cycle repeat itself for two decades, I am convinced that this is because people are focused on "getting in" when they should simply be committed to staying together. My hope is that you will keep it simple—love your kids well. They need to hear it, so do not stop telling them, "I trust you. And I am proud of you."

Soon (sooner than you probably want to believe) you will be helping your child move into college and taking the requisite family picture next to some iconic campus building or statue. I witness these family moments every year, and I can tell you there are three possible scenarios:

1. Everyone cries: Mom, Dad, student (sometimes even the younger sibling or random passerby flagged down to take the picture).

2. Parents cry, and the student scans the walkway to see how many people are coming that direction.

3. Nobody cries, but there are a few deep breaths, bitten lips, rapid "blinking," and conspicuous eye wiping, but no actual visible tears.

Inevitably, however, for the families falling into the third group, someone comes back a few hours later (after getting all the bags, boxes, and small electrical devices into the residence hall) and absolutely bawls. Make no mistake—on that day everyone cries.

As a parent, these are complicated, bittersweet tears. They are a mixture of joy and loss, tears filled with both love and pain, tears of pride and regret, tears that distinctly remember small kids on bikes or wearing backpacks that hung down to their knees, and tears that hope for a life impossible to fully imagine. They are tears for words spoken and unspoken. These tears bemoan the end of a chapter and celebrate the start of a new one.

We cannot guarantee you *where* your family will be standing that day, but the fact that you have read this book gives us all the confidence in the world that your move-in day is coming. Our hope is that you will be committed to *how* your family arrives on campus—truly together. To quote a very wise woman: "There is no 100-percent right way. Just make sure your kids always know you love them and that you are proud of them. Everything else will take care of itself."

Acknowledgments

We would like to express our immense gratitude for those who have taught and supported us in writing this book. First and foremost, our families, from whom we have learned that the power of unity, connection, and unconditional love is the foundation for a healthy, balanced, and fulfilling life. Our children—Andrew, Elizabeth, Rebecca, and Samuel—are constant reminders of the importance of purposeless play and the joy that can be found in living in the moment. We also feel fortunate to work at institutions that support both the professional and personal growth of faculty and staff, as well as encouraging engagement in the field of education well beyond campus. We are grateful for our Rhode Island friends for bringing us together and reminding us that it is "all about the kids" and to Denis Gainty, whose example of love for his children is the foundation on which this book was built. Finally, we owe huge thanks to Greg Britton and the team at Johns Hopkins University Press for believing in this project, recognizing the potential, and helping us stay true to our message of hope and unity.

BRENNAN

Deep thanks to my family—Timothy, Marjorie, Daron, Justin, Meredy, Katherine, Jessa, Sam, and Rebecca Barnard—whose unconditional love and support have allowed me to pursue my calling as an educator and who have constantly made me want to be a better person. You have instilled in me the value of togetherness and commitment to others. To the many faculty members at Westtown School, Franklin & Marshall College, and the University of Vermont for teaching me how to express myself and for giving me the foundation upon which to build a meaningful life. To Ken and Claire Grant, Paul and Laurie Hurd, and the Hyde School community for launching my career and helping me realize that my vocation is to work with young people at this important time of transition. To the Derryfield School and an amazing group of colleagues, past and present, for their friendship, inspiration, and for providing the time and resources to pursue my passion for writing. I am especially grateful to Bruce Berk, Sue Flagg, Jill Teeters, and Amanda Gagne for their patient editing and insightful feedback over the years. Thanks to my colleagues at Making Caring Common at the Harvard Graduate School of Education and my partners at US Performance Academy for their support and flexibility. To the amazing educators of ACCIS, NACAC, and the Character Collaborative, whose dedication to students and their families is inspiring. To the thousands of students and families with whom I have worked, who have taught me volumes about human nature, fear, hope, and unity. To Matthew Struckmeyer for his tireless wordsmithing and ability to cut to the heart of my message. To Sarah Rebick, Mike Schell, Chris Sacco, John Rigney, Dan Sacco, Bill Cote, Tim and Pam Neville, Alisa Barnard, Matt Hyde, Andy Strickler, Susan Tree, Lloyd Thacker, Ben Temple, Kortni Campbell, Kasey Ormiston, Nancy Aronie, Alan Haas, Allison Matlack, Susan Kennedy, Mike Morris, Jennie Freeman, Allie Foy, Shereem Herndon-Brown, Eric Mayer, and many, many others whose friendship, guidance, and love fills my life. Finally, to Rick Clark, whose thoughtfulness, support, depth, and collaboration has made this journey meaningful, joyful, and memorable.

RICK

To my incredibly, ridiculously, amazingly patient and loving wife, Amy, who models every day the person I want to be someday. My kids, Andrew and Elizabeth, for the poignant reminder that the most important things in life are simple—and for bringing ineffable joy, purpose, and pride. I'm beyond thankful for my parents and sister for instilling confidence and demonstrating unconditional love. To the leadership of Georgia Tech for giving me the space to innovate, create, and risk in the name of "Progress and Service." Inexpressible appreciation and respect for my longtime colleagues for their constant encouragement and support, especially Matt McLendon, Mary Tipton Woolley, Katie Faussemagne, George P. Burdell, Deborah Smith, Becky Tankersley, and the unbelievably talented, passionate, and committed teams I've had the chance to serve alongside. Go Jackets! WSTE. Leadership Georgia 2018 (Best Class Ever) for reminding me "we get to do this." To the All Souls congregation for years of care and community. Cheers to Clambake Nation ("Hi, Neighbor!"). A huge shoutout and mad props to the NACAC/SACAC family for inspiring me to speak, write, and lead in the name of students, access, educational progress, and equity. To Brennan for his collaboration, trust, and invaluable perspective and kindness. Lastly, to my brothers—TJ, Crewser, and the McCauley Street boys—who share a bond unbroken by time or place. Much love.

Suggested Further Reading

10% Happier: How I Tamed the Voice in My Head, Reduced Stress without Losing My Edge, and Found Self-Help That Actually Works—a True Story by Dan Harris (2014)

Acceptance: A Legendary Guidance Counselor Helps Seven Kids Find the Right Colleges—and Find Themselves by David L. Marcus (2010)

Age of Opportunity: Lessons from the New Science of Adolescence by Laurence Steinberg (2015)

Anxious Kids Anxious Parents: 7 Ways to Stop the Worry Cycle and Raise Courageous and Independent Children by Lynn Lyons and Reid Wilson (2013)

At What Cost? Defending Adolescent Development in Fiercely Competitive Schools by David L. Gleason (2017)

Brainstorm: The Power and Purpose of the Teenage Brain by Dan Siegel (2014)

College: What It Was, Is, and Should Be by Andrew Delbanco (2014)

College of the Overwhelmed: The Campus Mental Health Crisis and What to Do about It by Richard Kadison and Theresa Foy DiGeronimo (2004)

Colleges That Change Lives: 40 Schools That Will Change the Way You Think about Colleges by Loren Pope (2012)

Creating a Class: College Admissions and the Education of Elites by Mitchell Stevens (2007)

The Curse of the Good Girl: Raising Authentic Girls with Courage and Confidence by Rachel Simmons (2010)

David and Goliath: Underdogs, Misfits, and the Art of Battling Giants by Malcolm Gladwell (2015)

The End of American Childhood by Paula S. Fass (2016)

Excellent Sheep: The Miseducation of the American Elite and the Way to a Meaningful Life by William Deresiewicz (2015)

Far from the Tree: Parents, Children and the Search for Identity by Andrew Solomon (2012)

Fiske Guide to Colleges 2019 by Edward B. Fiske (2019)

The Gift of Failure: How the Best Parents Learn to Let Go so Their Children Can Succeed by Jessica Lahey (2016)

Give and Take: Why Helping Others Drives Our Success by Adam Grant (2013)

Grit: The Power of Passion and Perseverance by Angela Duckworth (2016)

A Hope in the Unseen: An American Odyssey from the Inner City to the Ivy League by Ron Suskind (1999)

How Children Succeed: Grit, Curiosity, and the Power of Character by Paul Tough (2012)

How to Raise an Adult: Break Free of the Overparenting Trap and Prepare Your Kid for Success by Julie Lythcott-Haims (2015)

Let Your Life Speak: Listening for the Voice of Vocation by Parker Palmer (1999)

Letting Go: A Parents' Guide to Understanding the College Years (6th ed.) by Karen Levin Coburn (2016)

Mindfulness for the Next Generation: Helping Emerging Adults Manage Stress and Lead Healthier Lives by Holly Rogers and Margaret Maytan (2012)

The Naked Roommate: And 107 Other Issues You Might Run into in College by Harlan Cohen (2017)

Our Kids: The American Dream in Crisis by Robert D. Putnam (2015)

The Overachievers: The Secret Lives of Driven Kids by Alexandra Robbins (2006)

The Paradox of Choice: Why More Is Less by Barry Schwartz (2004)

The Parents We Mean to Be: How Well-Intentioned Adults Undermine Children's Moral and Emotional Development by Richard Weissbourd (2010)

Pressured Parents, Stressed Out Kids by Wendy S. Grolnick and Kathy Seal (2008)

The Road to Character by David Brooks (2016)

Start with Why: How Great Leaders Inspire Everyone to Take Action by Simon Sinek (2009)

The Teenage Brain: A Neuroscientist's Survival Guide to Raising Adolescents and Young Adults by Frances E. Jensen and Amy Ellis Nutt (2015)

There Is Life after College: What Parents and Students Should Know about Navigating School to Prepare for the Jobs of Tomorrow by Jeffrey J. Selingo (2017)

Tribe: On Homecoming and Belonging by Sebastian Junger (2016)

Ungifted: Intelligence Redefined; The Truth about Talent, Practice, Creativity, and the Many Paths to Greatness by Scott Barry Kaufman (2015)

Where You Go Is Not Who You'll Be: An Antidote to the College Admissions Mania by Frank Bruni (2016)

Web Resources

COLLEGE SEARCH TOOLS

bigfuture.collegeboard.org

www.princetonreview.com

www.collegedata.com

www.collegeview.com

www.collegeraptor.com

www.unigo.com

VIRTUAL COLLEGE TOURS

CampusTours: www.campustours.com

E Campus Tours: www.ecampustours.com

YouVisit: www.youvisit.com

STANDARDIZED TESTING

Fair Test: www.fairtest.org

SAT: collegereadiness.collegeboard.org

Khan Academy SAT test prep: www.khanacademy.org

ACT: www.act.org

ACT Academy test prep: academy.act.org

FINANCIAL AID AND SCHOLARSHIPS

NACAC financial aid resources: www.nacacnet.org

Student Aid: studentaid.ed.gov

FastWeb: www.fastweb.com

Department of Education: studentaid.ed.gov

FinAid: www.finaid.org

NextStudent: www.nextstudentloans.com

Fast Web: www.fastweb.com

Going Merry: www.goingmerry.com

RaiseMe: www.raise.me

Sallie Mae: www.salliemae.com

Wired Scholars: www.wiredscholar.com

Scholarships.com: www.scholarships.com

Scholarshiphelp.org: www.scholarshiphelp.org

Studentawardsearch.com: www.studentawardsearch.com

Personal Finance Analyst Scholarships: www
.personalfinanceanalyst.com

GENERAL

ACT: www.act.org

Campus Safety / Crime Stats: ope.ed.gov/campussafety

College Board: www.collegeboard.com

Colleges That Change Lives: www.ctcl.com

Common Application: www.commonapp.org

Coalition Application: www.coalitionforcollegeaccess.org

Education Conservancy: www.educationconservancy.org

NACAC: www.nacacnet.org

NCAA: www.ncaa.org

Glossary

APPLICATION PLANS

Early Action (EA): A nonbinding admission plan with deadlines typically between mid-October and late November. EA decisions normally released in December or January.

Early Decision (ED): A binding agreement where a student will commit to enrolling if admitted. Many colleges offer two rounds of early decision: ED1, usually in early November, and ED2, in early January. A few colleges allow applicants to apply early decision on a rolling basis, meaning that at any time during the admission cycle an applicant can decide to enter into a binding agreement in consideration of their candidacy. Students can apply to other colleges simultaneously, through nonbinding plans.

priority applications: Also called VIP applications, "snap apps," "fast apps," and a range of other names, they refer to streamlined applications (prepopulating biographical information) designed to encourage students to apply early. In many cases, schools using these applications waive application fees and essay requirements.

priority deadlines: A decision plan (often November 30 or December 1) allowing a student to be considered in the school's first round of review. This is often found at large state systems, such as the University of California.

Regular Decision (RD): The standard admission plan with deadlines usually in early January or February and notification in late March.

Restrictive Early Action (REA) / Single Choice Early Action (SCEA): A hybrid admission plan allowing students to apply and receive decisions early under a nonbinding application. In doing so, they agree not to apply to another school under a binding ED plan at the same time.

rolling admission: Ongoing review of applications in order of submission. Admission offers are extended on a rolling basis until the spots are filled, at which time most schools will still accept applications for the wait list.

TESTING

ACT: A standardized test used in college admission, with four primary sections: reading, writing, science, and math. Each subscore has a maximum score of 36 and the highest total score composite a student can earn is a 36.

CEEB Code: College Entrance Examination Board Code assigned to each high school and college. This code will be listed on the high school profile and can be obtained from a school's guidance office or through searching online.

IELTS: A test of English as a foreign language that uses a nine-band scale to clearly identify levels of proficiency, from nonuser (band score 1) to expert (band score 9).

SAT: A standardized test used in college admission, with two primary sections: evidence-based reading and writing, and math. Each subscore has a maximum score of 800 for a total possible score of 1600.

SAT Subject Tests: One-hour subject-specific standardized tests used by a small subset of highly selective colleges and universities.

superscoring: The use of individual subscores from different test administrations to represent the highest combined score.

test flexible: The combination of individual subscores from different assessments (e.g., SAT math, ACT writing, AP biology) in consideration for admission.

test optional: Standardized test scores are not required for admission. Note: some colleges will require additional essays or other information if student is not submitting scores.

TOEFL: Test of English as a Foreign Language that measures reading, listening, speaking, and writing skills necessary to perform academic tasks. Each section has a maximum score of 30.

FINANCIAL AID

cost of attendance: The total cost for an academic year: the amount of money that a student will pay for a year of college, including tuition and fees, room and board, as well as average costs for books, supplies, transportation, and personal expenses. Reporting this is a federal requirement. Financial aid cannot exceed the cost of attendance.

CSS Profile: College Scholarship Service Financial Aid Form required by many (mostly private) colleges in addition to the FAFSA.

demonstrated need: Cost of attendance minus the Expected Family Contribution gives the student's demonstrated need.

Estimated Expected Family Contribution (EFC): The amount of money that the federal and institutional aid formulas determine a family can afford to pay for college.

FAFSA: Free Application for Federal Student Aid is a requirement for any form of federal financial aid, as well as state aid (in most cases). It is also used by many colleges/universities to determine eligibility for institutional (school-based) aid.

Federal Direct Loan: Federal loan for students (formerly known as the Stafford Loan).

Federal Work-Study Program (FWSP): A form of financial aid awarded to a student who demonstrates financial need through their FAFSA. Typically, this includes an on-campus job.

grant: Money awarded to a student in "gift aid." These awards come at no cost to the student and do not have to be paid back in the future. Often used interchangeably with "scholarship."

merit scholarships: Financial awards based on a student's achievement or potential (academic, athletic, artistic, etc.). Typically awarded by the college/university or private organizations. Merit scholarship is not need-based "gift aid" and does not need to be paid back.

need-aware admissions: A process of reviewing applicants for admission in which the student's ability to pay *is* taken into consideration.

need-based financial aid: A combination of federal, state, and institutional grants/scholarships, loans, and other financial assistance offered to a student based on their ability to pay for their education, as determined by the FAFSA (and the CSS Profile, for schools that use it).

need-blind admissions: A process of reviewing applicants for admission in which a student's ability to pay *is not* taken into consideration.

net price: The amount of money a student will pay out of pocket after financial aid.

Net Price Calculator: A federally mandated tool that each school has on their financial aid website. This resource allows families to see an estimated financial aid package for which they might be eligible.

Pell Grant: A federal grant based on "exceptional financial need" that does not have to be repaid.

PLUS Loan: A low-interest government loan for parents.

Subsidized Direct Loan: Federal loan available to students with financial need. Amount available to borrow is determined by year in school and may only go to meet demonstrated need.

tuition discounting: The process by which a college offsets its published tuition "sticker" price with institutional grant/scholarship aid. A school's *discount rate* is the ratio of total institutional grant aid relative to gross tuition/fees revenue.

unmet need: Also referred to as "gapping," the difference between a student's financial aid award (gift aid, work-study, need-based loans) and a student's demonstrated financial need. It is a practice colleges employ when they are unable to meet the full demonstrated need of all admitted students.

Unsubsidized Direct Loan: Federal loan available to students regardless of financial need. Amount available to borrow is determined by year in school.

DECISIONS

acceptance/admit: An offer of admission to a college or university.

conditional acceptance: An offer of admission to a college or university that is contingent upon certain steps a candidate must take or criteria they must fulfill in order to ultimately enroll.

deferral: A delayed admission decision for candidates who apply through early application plans. Often an updated transcript / academic form and/or an update on involvement is required or recommended when a student is deferred.

denial: An application for admission to a college or university is declined.

guaranteed transfer: An applicant is denied admission as a first-year student but is offered the option to transfer to the college (frequently as a second-year student) provided the student earns a specified GPA at another institution.

Spring/January acceptance: An offer of admission to a college or university with a second-semester start date. Often these offers include the opportunity to enroll in a college-sponsored program off campus (usually abroad) to earn credit during the first semester.

wait list: Neither an acceptance nor a denial, this means an applicant is potentially admissible but that the college will keep the student on hold in the applicant pool for later consideration based on enrollment numbers. The student must claim a spot on the college's wait list for later consideration—often after the National Deposit Deadline Day (May 1).

OTHER TERMS

admit rate: The percentage of applicants who are offered admission.

Coalition Application: A universal application for admission used by over 140 public and private colleges and universities.

Common Application: A universal undergraduate application for admission used by over 800 public and private colleges and universities.

demonstrated interest: An applicant's level of enthusiasm for or engagement with a college as shown through visits, communication, and other contact with the admission office. Some schools track these interactions closely and use them as a factor in admission decisions.

gap year: A yearlong break between high school and college allowing a student to travel, work, or explore a passion (language, sport, culture).

high school profile: A document developed by a high school to provide colleges with context for that school's curriculum, middle-50-percent test scores, grading policies, community, demographics, college enrollment, and other relevant information.

holistic admission: A method for reviewing applicants that accounts for a student's quality and achievement both inside and outside the classroom.

institutional priority: Goals set by the college that often drive admission decisions. These could be geographic, demographic, or curricular.

legacy: An applicant with a family connection to the college. Evaluation and definition of legacy varies by school.

melt: The number or percentage of students who pay their admission/enrollment deposit but do not ultimately enroll.

rigor: Degree of challenge demonstrated within a high school curriculum. Often relative to choices/options or overall applicant pool locally, statewide, or within an applicant pool.

search: A process by which colleges contact large numbers of students to elicit their interest in the institution.

yield: The percentage of students admitted who choose to enroll at that college.

References

Chapter 1. *Why* Are You Going to College?

Matthews, J. 2010. "No Easy Solution to the Mysteries of College Admissions." *Washington Post*, May 24, 2010. http://www.washingtonpost.com/wp-dyn /content/article/2010/05/23/AR2010052303569.html?noredirect=on.

Chapter 2. Remapping the Admission Landscape

Belyavina, R., J. Li, and R. Bhandari. 2013. "New Frontiers: U.S. Students Pursuing Degrees Abroad." Institute of International Education (website). https://www.iie.org/Research-and-Insights/Publications/New-Frontiers.

Clinedinst, M., and P. Patel. 2018. "State of College Admission." NACAC (website). https://www.nacacnet.org/globalassets/documents/publications/ research/2018_soca/soca18.pdf, p. 9.

Fast Facts. 2018. "Fast Facts." Institute of International Education (website). https://www.iie.org/en/Research-and-Insights/Open-Doors/Fact-Sheets-and -Infographics/Fast-Facts.

Grove, A. 2018. "A Comparison of the Big Ten Universities." *ThoughtCo*, October 1, 2018 https://www.thoughtco.com/comparison-of-the-big-ten -universities-786967.

Institute of International Education. 2018. "Number of International Students in the United States Reaches New High of 1.09 Million." Institute of International Education (website), November 13, 2018. https://www.iie.org /en/Why-IIE/Announcements/2018/11/2018-11-13-Number-of-International -Students-Reaches-New-High.

IPEDS Data Retrieval Center. 2016–2017. U.S. Department of Education, Institute of Education Sciences, National Center for Education Statistics. https://nces.ed.gov/ipeds/datacenter/InstitutionList.aspx.

NACAC College Openings Update. 2018. https://www.nacacnet.org/news --publications/Research/CollegeOpenings.

Ruffalo Noel Levitz. 2018. *2018 Cost of Recruiting an Undergraduate Student Report.* Cedar Rapids, IA: Ruffalo Noel Levitz. http://learn.ruffalonl.com/rs/395 -EOG-977/images/RNL_2018_Cost_of_Recruiting_Report_EM-005.pdf.

Statista. 2018. "Community Colleges in the United States—Statistics & Facts." https://www.statista.com/topics/3468/community-colleges-in-the-united -states/.

US Department of Education, National Center for Education Statistics. 2018. *Digest of Education Statistics, 2016* (NCES 2017-094). Table 105.50.

U.S. News and World Report. n.d. "Top 100—Lowest Acceptance Rates (2017)." https://www.usnews.com/best-colleges/rankings/lowest-acceptance-rate.

Chapter 3. Wedges of College Admission

Dobson, A. 2018. "By the Numbers: Student Scholarship Chances." *admitted* (NACAC blog), October 29, 2018. http://admitted.nacacnet.org/wordpress /index.php/2018/10/29/by-the-numbers-student-scholarship-chances/.

Duke University. n.d. "Cost & Financial Aid." Duke Admissions (website). https://admissions.duke.edu/application/aid.

Federal Student Aid. 2018. https://studentaid.ed.gov/sa/types/loans/plus.

The Institute for College Access and Success. 2017. "Student Debt and the Class of 2017." https://ticas.org/sites/default/files/pub_files/classof2017.pdf.

Korn Ferry. 2018. "High Demand, Low Reward: Salaries for 2018 College Graduates." May 14, 2018. https://www.kornferry.com/press/high-demand-low-reward-salaries-for-2018-college-graduates-flat-korn-ferry-analysis-shows.

Lutostanski, S. 2018. "The Compelling Case for Being an 'Intentionally Lazy' Parent." *Washington Post*, April 10, 2018. https://www.washingtonpost.com/news/parenting/wp/2018/04/10/the-compelling-case-for-intentional-laziness-parenting/.

Student Loan Hero. 2018. "A Look at the Shocking Student Loan Debt Statistics for 2018." https://studentloanhero.com/student-loan-debt-statistics/.

University of North Carolina–Chapel Hill. n.d. "Cost of Attendance." UNC Admissions (website). https://admissions.unc.edu/afford/cost-of-attendance/.

US Department of Education. 2018. "Net Price Calculator Center." College Cost (website). https://collegecost.ed.gov/netpricecenter.aspx.

Velez, E., and L. Horn. 2018. *Stats in Brief: What High Schoolers and Their Parents Know about Four-Year Tuition and Fees in Their State*. Washington, DC: US Department of Education. Institute of Education Sciences, National Center for Education Statistics. https://nces.ed.gov/pubs2019/2019404.pdf.

Chapter 4. Creating a College List

Morse, R., E. Brooks, and M. Mason. 2018. "How U.S. News Calculated the 2019 Best Colleges Rankings." *U.S. News and World Report*, September 9, 2018. https://www.usnews.com/education/best-colleges/articles/how-us-news-calculated-the-rankings.

Straumsheim, C. 2016. "Decision Time." Inside Higher Ed (website), August 16, 2016. https://www.insidehighered.com/news/2016/08/24/study-finds-students-benefit-waiting-declare-major.

Chapter 6. Admission Factors I

Board of Regents, State of Iowa. 2019. "Regent Admission Index (2019)." https://www.iowaregents.edu/institutions/higher-education-links/regent-admission-index/.

Cal State University–Fullerton. 2019. "Eligibility Index." https://catalog.fullerton.edu/mime/media/3/942/Eligibility+Index+Table.png.

Chronicle of Higher Education. 2019. "Less-Selective Colleges with the Highest and Lowest Retention Rates." January 13, 2019. https://www.chronicle.com/article/Less-Selective-Colleges-With/245453.

The Coalition for College. 2018. "About Us." Coalition for College Access (website). http://www.coalitionforcollegeaccess.org/about-us.html.

Common Application. 2019. "About Us." CommonApp (website). https://www.commonapp.org/about-us.

Dix, W. 2016. "Rethinking the Meaning of Colleges, Low Acceptance Rates." *Forbes*, May 24, 2016. https://www.forbes.com/sites/willarddix/2016/05/24 /rethinking-the-meaning-of-colleges-low-acceptance-rates/#26edbdb41dd0.

Georgia Tech, Institute Research and Planning. 2003. *Georgia Tech Factbook (2003)*. https://irp.gatech.edu/sites/default/files/documents/FactBook /FactBook_2003.pdf.

Georgia Tech, Institute Research and Planning. 2013. *Georgia Tech Factbook (2013)*. https://irp.gatech.edu/sites/default/files/documents/FactBook /FactBook_2013.pdf.

Hamilton College. 2018. "Standardized Testing Requirements." Hamilton College (website). https://www.hamilton.edu/admission/apply/requirements.

Chapter 8. Admission Decisions

Amherst College. n.d. Amherst Mission. https://www.amherst.edu/amherst -story/facts/mission.

Caltech. 2018. Caltech Mission. http://www.caltech.edu/content/mission -statement.

Georgia Institute of Technology. n.d. Georgia Tech Mission. https://irp.gatech .edu/gt-visionmission-statements.

Pennington, B. 2016. "The Admissions Ratio: The UNC Systems 82-18 Split." *Media Hub*, May 18, 2016. http://mediahub.unc.edu/university-ratio-unc -systems-82-18-split/.

University of North Carolina–Chapel Hill. 2018. "UNC–Chapel Hill Mission." UNC (website). https://www.unc.edu/about/mission/.

Chapter 10. Closing Letters

Jobs, S. 2005. "'You've Got to Find What You Love,' Jobs Says." Stanford University Commencement Address. *Stanford News*, June 14, 2005. https://news.stanford.edu/2005/06/14/jobs-061505/.

Index